BIRDS

OF BRITAIN AND EUROPE

■ FIELD ■

NATURALIST'S

■ LIBRARY ■

BIRDS

OF BRITAIN AND EUROPE

ANDREW CLEAVE

INTRODUCED BY

TONY SOPER

WHSMITH

EXCLUSIVE
· BOOKS ·

This edition produced exclusively for
W H Smith

Published in 1991 by Hamlyn Publishing Group Limited,
part of Reed International Books,
Michelin House,
81 Fulham Road,
London SW3 6RB

ISBN 0-600-57079-7

Produced by Mandarin Offset

Printed and bound in Hong Kong

Colour Artwork by Ian Willis
Line drawings by Norman Arlott
Maps first published in the *Hamlyn Guide to Birds of Britain and Europe*
Wintering areas are shown in blue; breeding areas in red and where the bird occurs all
year round in purple; migration areas are shown in yellow

Contents

Introduction
by Tony Soper

Birdwatching is a modified form of hunting. But whereas primitive hunters sought only to fill their bellies, present-day bird hunters tend to be looking for information and enjoyment in tracking their quarry. And it is useful to be able to put a name to the animal you're watching, whether it is your next door neighbour or a Blue-cheeked Bee-eater. This guide serves the valuable purpose of helping to put a name to the bird, but it goes much further, in outlining its character, movements and habitat.

There is, of course, a severely practical and essential relationship between birds and men. Quite apart from their value as a primary food source, they are natural controllers of agricultural 'pests', agents for the propagation and pollination of plants, and so on. But there is more to it than that. Their songs liven up the spring, their colour and movement enrich the landscape all through the year. They come in all shapes and sizes, and those shapes and sizes have been achieved after a long process of trial and error, so they represent supreme fitness for purpose. Beaks, for instance. A sparrow has a powerful nutcracker bill, and is an expert at husking corn and other seeds. A Robin has a delicate probing bill which seeks and destroys soft grubs and worms. Ducks' feet are for paddling, Blue Tits' feet are for grasping. And so on. Just by having a good look at an animal we ought to be able to say something about the way it lives, even if we've never seen it before and don't know what kind of country it inhabits.

The power of flight gives birds the key to world travel. A tern may spend the summer nesting in the Arctic, then strike south to 'winter' in the Antarctic, incredible though that may seem to us. From its point of view it is simply making the best of both worlds and enjoying perpetual summer. Not all birds use those feathers to propel them across the world. Flight has other values. Instant escape from enemies, airborne invasion of an area rich in caterpillars, or fast approach and capture of prey; all these things are possible with feathers. And different bird have different designs to fit them best for different purposes. A Swift has narrow, swept-back wings, designed for speed and aerial fly-chasing; its take-off and landing performance is poor. A Pheasant has broad, short wings, giving a powerful near-vertical take off for instant escape, although it pays for the facility by having low endurance, needing to land again within a short distance – far enough away, though, to keep out of trouble.

Even for flightless birds, which might at first seem to make nonsense of all those years of research and development, the wings are important pieces of equipment. A penguin's flipper may seem an un-feather-like, hard, rigid structure, but it is in fact a modified wing superbly built for flying underwater; the bird is a master submariner.

Birds have a great sense of adventure, which appeals to us. They will go anywhere, try anything, and have an aptitude for taking advantage of any situation. So it's not surprising that many of them have learnt the benefits of a close association with man.

Kestrels patrol the motorway verges for voles to feed their chicks on the ledges of high-rise flats. Robins follow the gardener's spade, pigeons join the lunch-time sandwich-eaters, gulls haunt the rubbish tip.

One way and another, these feathered animals have an awesome ability to make a living wherever there's a living to be made. Where there's anything edible there's a bird in every field – in the air, in the desert and at sea. They pursue a variety of ingenious lifestyles. And quite as interesting as any of the far-flung adventurers are the birds which live next door to us. You will never be bored once you take an interest in ornithology, for you only have to see a bird to begin asking any number of questions. What is its name? Where does it come from and why? What does it eat and how does it find its food? What are its relations with you, me and its fellows? This book helps you find the answers.

Tony Soper

STRUCTURE OF A BIRD

The bodies of birds are adapted to flight and almost every feature, such as the skeleton, respiratory and circulatory systems, digestive tract, reproductive organs and the feathers, shows an adaptation to flight.

Feathers

The feature which immediately separates birds from other vertebrates is the body covering of feathers. These are of four basic types: flight feathers, down and semi-plume feathers and filoplumes. Body feathers cover most of the body and provide its streamlined shape and give insulation. They also provide the body with its characteristic colourings or camouflage. Flight feathers are the large feathers of the wings and tail. They are similar to the body feathers but are larger and stronger. Down feathers are short and soft, and are found below the body feathers. They provide insulation and are especially important in water birds and those living in very cold climates.

Filoplumes are hair-like and sometimes have a downy tuft at the tip and are found amongst the other feathers. They are linked with sensitive cells which help the bird judge how the feathers are lying on its body.

Some insectivorous birds have stiff bristles around the bill which may help sense the position of their insect prey, and some have bristles around their eyes, possibly for protection.

Small birds have fewer feathers than larger birds. The Blue Tit has about 1,500 feathers, but the Mute Swan has about 25,000. The numbers on an individual vary according to its state of moult.

Moulting

Feathers become worn and faded, losing their strength and efficiency, so twice each year they are replaced when the bird moults. In some species moulting takes place gradually, but in others, such as some species of waterbirds, all the flight feathers are lost at the same time and the bird becomes flightless for a while. Some wildfowl, like Eider and Shelduck, congregate in large flocks to moult. In some species, birds may change colour when they moult, having a different set of feathers and a different appearance for winter and summer.

Males of many species have elaborate colourings in the summer during

Skeleton of a pigeon

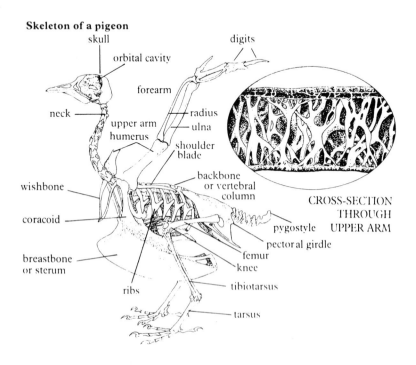

skull

orbital cavity

digits

forearm

neck

upper arm
humerus

radius
ulna

shoulder
blade

backbone
or vertebral
column

wishbone

coracoid

pygostyle

pectoral girdle

femur

knee

tibiotarsus

breastbone
or sterum

ribs

tarsus

CROSS-SECTION
THROUGH
UPPER ARM

Cormorant drying its wings

the breeding season, but look more like the females in winter after they have moulted. Juvenile birds often look different from their parents, having camouflaged markings for protection, and only take on adult colourings after their first moult.

Feather care

Birds spend a lot of time preening, or caring for their feathers. The barbs which may have become unlocked during flight are linked back together by fine nibbling movements with the bill and parasites are removed. Oil from the preen gland above the base of the tail is spread over the feathers, and bathing takes place whenever possible to remove dust. Scratching also takes place during preening and may be caused by irritating parasites like fleas or feather lice. Some birds enjoy dust bathing and probably do this to rid the skin of parasites. Some species allow ants to crawl over their bodies; this strange behaviour may also help rid them of parasites or prevent infestations by lice.

Wing structure

A bird's wing is designed to create lift and produce forward movement. As it beats downwards the wing twists slightly, pushing the air down and away from the bird; the result is that the bird is pushed in the opposite direction. In order to smooth the airflow over the wing when the bird slows down, the alula or bastard wing is raised. The tips of the primary feathers are spread in some birds, such as Partridges and Buzzards, in order to reduce the loss of lift at the tip of their rounded wings.

Great Spotted Woodpecker in flight

Flight patterns

Gliding flight is achieved by birds with long wings. The Fulmar has long, slender wings which can maximise the air currents over the sea and in wave troughs. Kites and Buzzards have broader wings which can utilise up-draughts and give manoeuvrability. Pheasants have shorter, rounded wings and long tails which enable them to make short explosive bursts of flight, rising rapidly to escape from danger; this can only be sustained for a short time and the bird soon glides back to ground. Auks use their wings as paddles underwater, but have to beat them rapidly in the air in order to stay airborne; they are short in relation to the body length. Birds which can make short, powerful bursts of flight in confined places like woodlands are often less efficient at flying for long periods in the open and have an undulating flight like woodpeckers.

Other means of movement

Some birds, like auks, are very well adapted to swimming and can pursue their prey underwater using their wings as paddles. Diving ducks use their feet to propel themselves and some use the folded wing as well. Terns do not swim underwater but dive below the surface from a height. Ducks and wildfowl swim well on the surface and can also walk well on land, but they are usually unable to propel themselves below the surface. Woodpeckers and treecreepers have claws which enable them to cling onto trees and run up and down them. Some small woodland birds are efficient at hanging upside down on branches and twigs in search of food. Birds which feed on the ground are generally good at running, although a few species seem only to be able to hop. Waders, pipits and larks walk and run efficiently, but finches and thrushes, which may spend some of their time in trees, tend to hop on the ground.

Feeding

A bird's beak indicates what type of food it eats. All birds have the same basic type of beak with a fixed upper mandible and a more flexible lower mandible. The outer surface of the bill is covered with a horny layer of a material called keratin, similar to our fingernails. Thrushes have a general purpose bill which enables them to

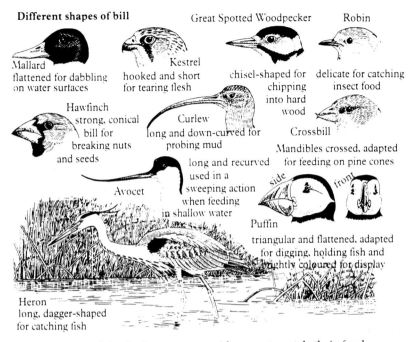

Different shapes of bill

Great Spotted Woodpecker

Robin

Mallard
flattened for dabbling
on water surfaces

Kestrel
hooked and short
for tearing flesh

chisel-shaped for
chipping
into hard
wood

delicate for catching
insect food

Hawfinch
strong, conical
bill for
breaking nuts
and seeds

Curlew
long and down-curved for
probing mud

Crossbill

Mandibles crossed, adapted
for feeding on pine cones

Avocet

long and recurved
used in a
sweeping action
when feeding
in shallow water

side   front

Puffin

triangular and flattened, adapted
for digging, holding fish and
brightly coloured for display

Heron
long, dagger-shaped
for catching fish

feed on a variety of foods, but many species are more specialised. Tits have smaller bills which are able to catch tiny insects, but also strong enough to tap away at seeds and open them. Finches have stronger bills which can crack open seeds and are provided with grooves which enable them to hold the seed in place. Birds of prey have strong muscles and hooked beaks which enable them to tear at their prey, and in some cases to kill it. Wading birds have longer bills which can probe mud in search of food and in some cases they have sensitive tips to help locate the food. A few waders have shorter bills used to pick food from the surface, but the Snipe has a bill as long as its body with a flexible tip so that it can catch its prey when the bill is pushed deep into mud. Ducks mostly have broader bills needed to filter mud or grasp vegetation. Fish-eaters usually have finely-serrated edges to the mandibles which help them to grasp slippery prey. The smallest and least powerful bills are found in the insect-feeders such as swifts and martins which rely on a wide gape to catch their food.

The bird's digestive tract differs from that of mammals in that it has a crop and a gizzard. The crop is used to store food in temporarily and does not digest it. It enables birds to collect a large amount of food very quickly and then fly off to a safe place to digest it more slowly. The gizzard takes the place of teeth and grinds food down into smaller particles which can be digested in the stomach and intestines. Seed eaters collect grit which remains in the gizzard and helps break down the food.

Claws

A bird's feet and claws are often as distinctive as its beak, indicating once again its method of feeding and its way of movement. Swimming and diving birds generally have webbed feet, but some, like the Coot and Great Crested Grebe have lobes between the toes. Waders and herons normally have long toes which help distribute their weight over mud. Birds of prey are provided with sharp claws and powerful leg muscles so that they can grip their prey. Finches, thrushes, tits and warblers are 'perching birds', and as well as being able to walk or hop on the ground are able to perch on thin branches. Woodpeckers have claws which grip easily onto wood, enabling them to anchor themselves on the tree while they hammer into bark with their strong bills.

BREEDING

The egg of a bird contains a rich supply of food for the developing embryo. Eggs are produced singly by the female as it would be difficult to carry several large eggs and still be able to fly. When a clutch is complete, incubation begins and the development of the embryo commences.

All the eggs in a clutch hatch at the same time, except in those species, such as owls, which start incubation as soon as the first egg is laid. Some species, such as Guillemots and Razorbills, lay a single egg and are unable to replace it if it is lost more than a few days after it was laid. Thrushes usually lay a clutch of four eggs and some wildfowl, like the Mallard, can lay a clutch of 12 or more eggs.

In order to protect the developing eggs and young birds, most species build nests, often concealing them in thick vegetation or tree holes, or build them in inaccessible places like high tree tops or cliff faces. A few species use old nests of other birds; Long-eared Owls often lay their eggs in an old Crow's nest. Some seabirds use no nesting material at all, laying their eggs on bare rock and relying on their own bodies as the only means of protecting the chick.

Ground nesting species like gamebirds often produce young which are able to run almost as soon as they hatch, and follow the parents to safety. Some species, like warblers and tits, produce young which are helpless and must be protected in the nest for almost as long as they were developing in the egg. Their nests are often very well concealed. In the case of some birds of prey and owls, in which the young hatch at intervals, the oldest young may eat its younger brothers and sisters if food is scarce so that it receives an adequate supply of food, ensuring that at least one bird survives.

12

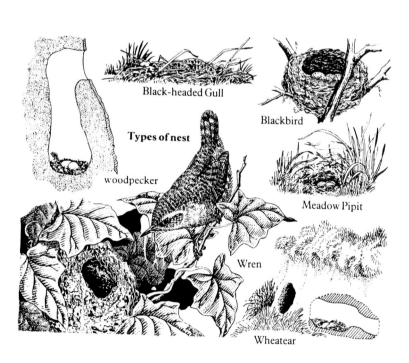

Black-headed Gull

Blackbird

Types of nest

woodpecker

Meadow Pipit

Wren

Wheatear

The Swallow is a well-known long distance migrant

Reproduction is an exhausting process and some species, like many of the seabirds are able to produce only one brood of young in a year, but others, like Blackbirds and Wood Pigeons may produce several broods in a year, starting very early in the season and continuing for as long as there is food and fine weather.

MIGRATION

The ability to fly has enabled birds to cover great distances and reach every continent in the world. Some species regularly make long migrations in order to reach breeding grounds which offer safe nesting sites and good feeding, and then return to different winter quarters. Vast journeys may be undertaken every year and long-lived species like terns may cover a greater distance in their lives than any other living creature. Swallows fly from northern Europe to southern Africa, crossing mountains, seas and desert during the course of a very long and hazardous journey.

It is thought that birds use the position of the sun and stars to help them find their way whilst migrating. Some species travel at night and may become lost if the weather is bad, or they may fly towards a lighthouse or gas flare. Species which fly during the day probably use landmarks like the coastline or valleys to help find their way.

They try to avoid making long sea crossings and vast numbers of birds from Europe cross the Mediterranean Sea into Africa at the Straits of Gibraltar, across the island of Sicily, or into Asia across the Bosphorous. They are then faced with long desert crossings and need to build up good food reserves before continuing the journey. Millions of birds die on the journey, many of them facing natural hazards like storms, drought or starvation, but in some countries, like Italy, millions of migrating birds are shot and trapped for 'sport'.

BIRDWATCHING

Birds can be seen almost anywhere – even in the middle of a large town. Sometimes they are not afraid of people and can be observed closely. Bird tables attract a variety of species to gardens where they can be watched from a window. In order to get good views of most species of birds, however, binoculars will be a great help.

A very good pair of binoculars can be expensive, but cheaper models can be found which are quite acceptable. Try out several pairs and check for the quality of the lenses. Look at an object which you know to be upright, such as a telegraph pole or the edge of a building and test the binoculars to see if they distort. Check also that they do not cause 'colour fringing' and give strange halos to the outlines of birds. On the top of the binoculars near the lens will be two figures such as '8 x40'. The first figure refers to the magnification - anything over 10 or below 7 will not be very useful for birdwatching. The second figure refers to the diameter of the objective lens, the larger of the lenses. This lens admits the light so it is important that it is of good quality and of sufficient size. Anything smaller then 40mm diameter will not gather sufficient light for birdwatching in poor light conditions, such as at dusk or in dark woodland. Divide the lens diameter by the magnification to get the 'exit pupil diameter' of the binoculars. A pair of 8 x 40 binoculars give a figure of 5 which is good, but a pair of 8 x 30 binoculars give a figure of 3.75 which is not quite good enough for birdwatching. Aim for a figure of about 5 if possible.

Notes and diagrams

Making notes about a strange bird and sketching its key features will help you to learn more about it and identify it correctly. It is important that you do this before you refer to a field guide as this could influence what you note down. You can check your notes against diagrams in a field guide at a later time and decide on the bird's identity. Always make a note of the date, time and the location as these will also be of help. Note down any special features of the bird's behaviour such as its flight pattern, how it moves on the ground or feeds, and its call.

14

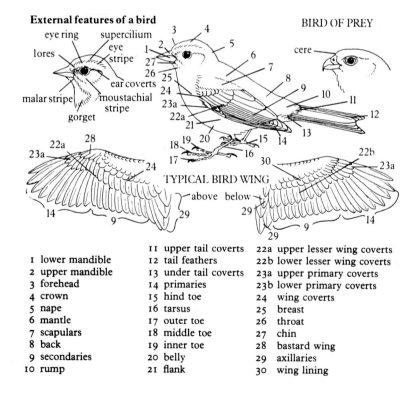

External features of a bird

BIRD OF PREY

TYPICAL BIRD WING

1 lower mandible	11 upper tail coverts	22a upper lesser wing coverts
2 upper mandible	12 tail feathers	22b lower lesser wing coverts
3 forehead	13 under tail coverts	23a upper primary coverts
4 crown	14 primaries	23b lower primary coverts
5 nape	15 hind toe	24 wing coverts
6 mantle	16 tarsus	25 breast
7 scapulars	17 outer toe	26 throat
8 back	18 middle toe	27 chin
9 secondaries	19 inner toe	28 bastard wing
10 rump	20 belly	29 axillaries
	21 flank	30 wing lining

Keeping a diary of bird sightings can be very useful as it helps to build up a picture of bird movements, migration times, and breeding habits. This information may also be of use when surveys into bird populations are being conducted.

In the field

Always consider the safety of the birds when birdwatching and do nothing which will disturb or harm them, especially during the breeding season. It is important for the birdwatcher to keep as quiet as possible; in this way the birds will not be disturbed and will behave more naturally. Learn to move quietly and not make sudden appearances over banks or in openings in hedges; birds are easily startled and one scared bird may make an alarm call which will alert many others.

Clubs and societies

Joining a birdwatching club is an excellent way of getting to know the best places to go birdwatching, and more experienced members will be able to help with identification. Clubs often organise surveys of local areas and well-kept diaries and note-books will be of great benefit here.

CONSERVATION

Many species of birds are endangered and are in urgent need of conservation. Although nearly all species are protected by law from shooting and disturbance, many are still declining, mainly through loss of their habitats. Important habitats such as estuaries are constantly under threat from major developments. Woodland and hedgerow clearance, pesticide poisoning, oil pollution at sea, illegal trapping and poisoning all account for the losses of birds, so it is important for birdwatchers to keep a constant watch out for threats to the survival of our birds.

The Red-backed Shrike was once a fairly widespread bird in southern Britain, but now is hardly ever seen there; climatic changes may explain why it has declined, but its favourite heathland habitat is no longer as common, so we must ensure that no other species suffer the same decline through loss of their vital feeding and breeding areas. We know the reasons for the decline of many bird species; the responsibility for the survival of the birds and their habitats is ours.

15

A group of birdwatchers out for the day along a stretch of coast

ROCKY CLIFFS, COASTS AND ESTUARIES

Sea cliffs are breeding places for a great variety of seabirds which make use of the safety of the cliffs for their nests and the sea for food. Many different species may be present on a single cliff with some of them occurring in impressive numbers.

Each species has its own preference for nest sites so overall numbers on one cliff can be very high. Cliffs with exposed rocks lying in horizontal strata are very suitable for ledge-nesting species like Guillemots and Kittiwakes. Caves and crevices suit Razorbills and Black Guillemots and loose scree and soft soil which can be burrowed into are ideal for Manx Shearwaters and Puffins. Gulls nest on cliff tops and larger ledges and Cormorants prefer to be nearer the sea on large rocks at the base of the cliff.

Competition for nesting sites is so great in some seabird colonies that birds arrive to take up territories at the end of winter, long before the breeding season begins. Some seabirds, like Gannets, nest in vast colonies of a single species, and may be present in tens of thousands. The cliffs are often covered with a thick layer of white guano, or bird droppings. A visit to a seabird colony in the height of the breeding season is one of the most impressive sights on the coast.

Sandy coasts are also very important for coastal birds as they provide nesting sites for terns, gulls and waders and offer an abundance of food. Many sandy beaches are important recreational areas and are subject to constant disturbance, but those that are protected in nature reserves are very valuable as nesting and feeding areas. Wading birds show many adaptations to feeding in mud, and like the nesting birds on cliffs, several different species may be present in one area, all exploiting different foods with their variety of feeding methods.

Oil pollution at sea is seriously affecting seabird populations and some species have shown a marked decline this century, but commercial fisheries have benefitted some species.

A large Gannet colony on Bass Rock, Scotland

17

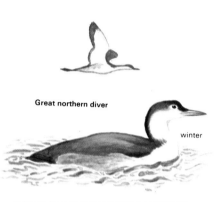

Great northern diver

winter

GREAT NORTHERN DIVER
Gavia immer L70-80cm
Characteristics: A large diving bird with striking black and white summer plumage; the head is black, the neck has alternate black and white bands and the back is spotted. The white underside is seen during its 'roll-preening' on the water. In winter the back is dark without spots and the neck is white with a contrasting black head. A sad-sounding wailing song is heard over the breeding area and a goose-like 'kwuk-kwuk-kwuk' call in flight.

18

Distribution and habitat: Breeds on large freshwater lakes, especially if they have small islands in them, in Iceland and Greenland, but is widespread along the coast, and sometimes on large inland lakes and reservoirs, in winter.

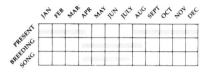

Habits and similar species: Dives for fish from the surface of the water and swims well, but is ungainly on land and rarely comes ashore. May be confused with the White-billed Diver, *Gavia adamsii*, which has an all yellowish-white bill with more pointed and tip-tilted appearance.

Black-throated diver

summer

BLACK-THROATED DIVER
Gavia arctica L60-70cm
Characteristics: Grey head in summer with black throat-patch and vertical black and white stripes on side of neck distinguish it from Great Northern Diver. Slightly smaller bill and sloping forehead also help separate the two species. Its deep 'kwok-kwok' call is similar to the Great Northern Diver and its mournful wailing song may also cause confusion. In winter the crown and back of neck appear paler than the dark back.

Distribution and habitat: Breeds on large freshwater lakes in northern Britain and Scandinavia, moving to the coast for the winter where local concentrations may build up in good feeding areas. Some may travel as far as the Mediterranean and Black and Caspian Seas.

Habits and similar species: Dives for fish from the surface, swimming well and flying powerfully if necessary. May be confused with larger Great Northern Diver in winter but its paler head and darker back may help separate them.

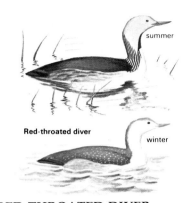

Red-throated diver

summer

winter

Distribution and habitat: Breeds on shallow lochs and tarns in northern Britain, Scandinavia and Iceland, making a scrape-like nest at the water's edge. It has left some areas because of disturbance. In winter may be found along most coasts and some large inland waters.

RED-THROATED DIVER
Gavia stellata L50-60cm
Characteristics: The commonest and smallest diver, identified in the breeding season by the red throat patch with grey sides and vertical black and white stripes at the back. Winter plumage is grey with light speckling on the back and a paler face than other divers. The red eye is sometimes seen, but the slightly up-turned appearance of the bill is distinct. Its eerie call is far-carrying and its duck-like flight note is heard as birds circle before settling.

Habits and similar species: Dives for fish from the surface, sometimes quite close inshore, and may form large scattered flocks in winter in good feeding areas. May be confused with large grebes, such as Red-necked and Great Crested, but larger, up-turned appearance of bill, and dark trailing edge of wing with no white wing bar distinguish it.

19

Distribution and habitat: Common around all coasts with nesting ledges, usually in colonies; may be seen on buildings many miles inland when coastal nest-sites are scarce. In winter they disperse over the sea, often following fishing boats for discarded fish scraps.

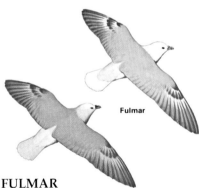

Fulmar

FULMAR
Fulmarus glacialis L47cm
Characteristics: A gull-like petrel with greyish upperparts and a white head and body. Its stiff-winged, gliding flight and more compact body distinguish it from large gulls. The wings lack black tips and the eye appears large due to a dark spot behind it. The tube-like nostrils and hooked tip to the bill are typical of all petrels. Arctic birds may be almost all greyish-blue, and rarely, a pure white form can be seen. Cackling calls may be heard from birds on the nest.

Habits and similar species: Intruders to the nest are attacked with a vile-smelling oil which the Fulmars spit at them, and the birds may spend many hours gliding past a possible nesting ledge trying to land on it, only to be repelled by another bird. In poor light dark birds may be confused with the Manx Shearwater far out to sea as both species glide over the waves with very few wing beats.

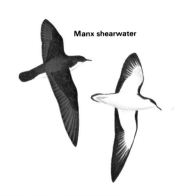

Manx shearwater

MANX SHEARWATER
Puffinus puffinus L35cm

Characteristics: The contrast between the dark upperparts and the white underside, coupled with the effortless gliding flight over the waves, make it easy to recognise at sea, but it is rarely seen on land due to its nocturnal habits. Its legs are set far back on the body to help it swim, so it is unable to walk, except in a shuffling fashion. Its loud wailing, screeching calls can be heard at night at breeding colonies.

Distribution and habitat: Manx Shearwaters nest on rocky islands on western coasts, using deep burrows, sometimes on cliffs very far above sea level. Outside the breeding season they disperse far out into the Atlantic.

	JAN	FEB	MAR	APR	MAY	JUN	JULY	AUG	SEPT	OCT	NOV	DEC
PRESENT												
BREEDING												
SONG												

Habits and similar species: Shearwaters catch their food at the sea surface, sometimes making shallow, splashy dives. Fishing trips may take them far from the breeding colony for days, but their remarkable powers of navigation help them relocate their own nesting burrows easily. The Mediterranean race is browner above, and the Sooty Shearwater is all dark, apart from a paler band on the underwing.

STORM PETREL
Hydrobates pelagicus L15cm

Characteristics: Very small, black, with a white rump. Dark bill has tube nostrils and slightly hooked tip. Flies low over the water with dark feet trailing and picks small items of food from the surface. Often follows fishing boats for scraps. Only seen on land during breeding season. Strange churring call ending in a 'hiccup' is heard near nesting burrows.

Distribution and habitat: Nests on rocky islands and steep cliffs in burrows and crevices, only coming ashore at night. Winters far out to sea, south of the main breeding range, but may be driven ashore by gales. May form small flocks and follow fishing boats.

	JAN	FEB	MAR	APR	MAY	JUN	JULY	AUG	SEPT	OCT	NOV	DEC
PRESENT												
BREEDING												
SONG												

Habits and similar species: Small size, fluttering flight and habit of picking food from the surface without alighting make Storm Petrels easy to identify, but Leach's Petrel is similar with forked tail and paler wing bar; its flight is more buoyant and erratic in direction. Migrating House Martins may also cause confusion, but they are unlikely to be flying low over the water, and never pick food from the surface.

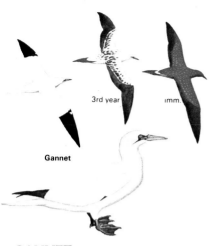

Distribution and habitat: Gannets breed on rocky islands and steep mainland cliffs, sometimes in huge colonies. A population expansion in recent years has led to new colonies being formed. In winter they disperse far out to sea and are rarely seen near land.

GANNET
Sula bassana L90cm
Characteristics: The largest seabird of the area with a wingspan of nearly 200cm. Its white plumage and striking black wing-tips make it easy to pick out. At closer range its yellowish head and blue eyes can be seen. The bluish-grey bill is massive and pointed. Juveniles are spotted dark brown and white becoming whiter with age.

Habits and similar species: Gannets dive steeply into the sea from a great height to capture their prey which is usually large fish like herring and mackerel. Large flocks of birds quickly gather if shoals of fish are spotted. At the breeding colony they are noisy and aggressive, stabbing fiercely at intruders, but mated pairs indulge in a peaceful 'sky-pointing' display.

21

Distribution and habitat: A common breeding bird on most rocky coasts, usually found in large colonies, often near other nesting seabirds. In the winter present around the coast, rarely straying inland, and not usually very far out to sea.

SHAG
Phalacrocorax aristotelis L76cm
Characteristics: All-dark with a beautiful green gloss to the summer plumage. Eye is a deep bottle green with a yellow ring; base of the bill is also yellow. In the breeding season a prominent forward-pointing crest is present. Juveniles light brown with a paler chin and throat and darker eyes. The deep, guttural croaking call is heard mainly at the breeding colony.

Habits and similar species: Dives for fish and crustaceans from the surface, often re-appearing with the prey visible in its bill. Bill held pointing upwards when on the water, and wings often held out to dry when on land. Smaller than Cormorant, but can be confused in winter and at great distance. Longer tail and upwards pointing head differentiate it from divers on the water.

CORMORANT
Phalacrocorax carbo L90cm
Characteristics: A large dark seabird with long neck and powerful, straight, hook-tipped bill. In the breeding season the throat and thighs are white. Juveniles are brown above, paler below. Loud guttural croaking calls heard at breeding colonies.

Distribution and habitat: Nests around the coast on rocky islands and cliffs, but also uses man-made sites such as dock-side

buildings and occasionally in trees by freshwater. In winter disperses around the coast; often in estuaries or on large lakes and reservoirs far from the sea.

Habits and similar species: Spends much of its time sitting on posts or buoys over the water, often with wings outstretched. Dives from the surface for fish, often surfacing with large prey like flatfish. Larger than Shag and with more massive bill, and more often seen on freshwater. The upwards pointing head, longer tail and arched back when diving distinguishes this species from the divers.

EIDER
Somateria mollissima L58cm
Characteristics: A large sea duck with a heavy wedge-shaped bill. The male has striking black and white plumage; no other drake is white above and black below. The crown and tail are black but the back of the head has beautiful pale green markings and the breast is pale pink. 'Cooing' courtship call heard in spring. Females are brown with darker brown barrings on the breast. Immature and moulting males have a varied black and white plumage, but usually with black crown and black underparts.

Distribution and habitat: Breed on rocky and sandy coasts in northern Britain, Iceland and Scandinavia, usually in colonies

close to sea level. In winter, they move south from the most northerly breeding areas, but always stay close to the shore finding mussel beds to feed on.

Habits and similar species: Moulting males form large flocks offshore in summer while females form creches with their young. Both sexes dive for large molluscs such as mussels, but females teach young to collect smaller shells at first. King Eider male has red bill and a blue crown and nape, but females are very similar; female King Eider shows pale eye-ring and has slightly smaller bill.

flock

♂

Common scoter

♀

COMMON SCOTER
Melanitta nigra L48cm
Characteristics: An all-dark sea-duck with an orange patch on the upper surface of the bill. Females are brown with pale cheek patches and darker crown. Juveniles also have pale cheeks and belly. The piping call, which can carry long distances, is occasionally heard near the breeding grounds.

Distribution and habitat: Breeds near lakes or large slow rivers in northern Britain; Iceland and Scandinavia in moorland and tundra. May form colonies in suitable areas. In winter, huge flocks gather off coasts south of main breeding range; some wander inland.

Habits and similar species: Dives from the surface for small molluscs and crustaceans, taking insect larvae in summer, feeding on freshwater lakes. Its nest, usually concealed in low vegetation, is lined with down from the female. Male may be confused with Velvet Scoter, which has small white patch behind eye, white wing bar and red feet. Female similar to Velvet Scoter and Red-crested Pochard.

23

Great skua

GREAT SKUA
Stercorarius skua L58cm
Characteristics: A bulky dark-brown gull-like seabird, showing conspicuous white wing-flashes in flight and especially during its territorial display when the bird stands near its nest site with wings held above the body and gives a harsh barking call. The plumage is all brown and the legs, bill and eyes are dark.

Distribution and habitat: Breed on moorland, usually near the sea and colonies of other seabirds, which they will prey on. In winter they disperse out to sea, but during migration they are often seen near the coast following and harrying other migrating seabirds.

Habits and similar species: Skuas feed by terrorising other birds and stealing their food. They may also attack and kill smaller seabirds, eat young skuas if they stray from the nest, and scavenge, especially around fishing boats where they compete with large gulls and Fulmars. Males defend territories against all intruders, including humans, by an intimidating flight attack.

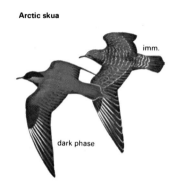

Arctic skua

imm.

dark phase

ARCTIC SKUA
Stercorarius parasiticus L46cm
Characteristics: Smaller and slimmer than the Great Skua, with a more dashing flight reminiscent of a falcon. The dark crown contrasts with the body, even in birds showing a dark coloration. The wings are always a dark greyish-brown with striking white wing-flashes. A yelping call is heard on the breeding grounds and sometimes whilst pursuing another bird.

24

Distribution and habitat: Breed in northern Britain, Iceland and Scandinavia on moorland near the sea and cliff-tops near seabird colonies. When other seabirds are migrating they follow them, and in winter they disperse over a vast area, rarely coming close to the shore.

Habits and similar species: The falcon-like flight enables Arctic Skuas to pursue other sea-birds, especially birds returning to a breeding colony with food for their young, and make them drop it; the food item is then caught in mid-air. The Pomarine Skua has twisted, blunt-ended central tail feathers and a dark bar across the breast. The Long-tailed Skua has much longer central tail feathers.

Herring gull

2nd summer

HERRING GULL
Larus argentatus L60cm
Characteristics: Large, with silver-grey wings and contrasting black wing tips showing white spots. The legs are pink, but birds from the Mediterranean have yellow legs. Juveniles brown in first year, moulting into adult plumage by the third summer. Large yellow bill has an orange spot on lower mandible. Many calls, from the familiar mewing cry to a more aggressive 'kee-ouw'.

Distribution and habitat: A common breeding bird around all coasts and also in some inland areas, nesting on the ground, on cliffs and often on buildings. More coastal in winter, but some birds form large roosts on reservoirs, moving to refuse tips to scavenge during the day.

Habits and similar species: A great opportunist, feeding in a wide range of habitats and on a variety of foods. The large bill can be used to tear up large food items, and eggs and chicks can be gulped down in raids on other birds' nests. The much larger Glaucous Gull has silver wings, but lacks the black wing tips, and the similar-sized Iceland Gull also has silver-grey wings without the contrasting tips.

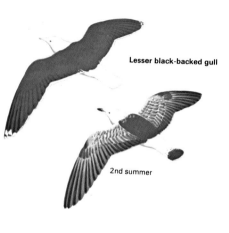

Lesser black-backed gull

2nd summer

Distribution and habitat:
Breeds on all coasts, moving south for winter from the northern part of its range. Nests colonially on

the ground on islands, dunes, cliffs, sometimes just inland. May join other gulls on lakes and reservoirs, otherwise winters south to Mediterranean.

	JAN	FEB	MAR	APR	MAY	JUN	JULY	AUG	SEPT	OCT	NOV	DEC
PRESENT												
BREEDING												
SONG												

LESSER BLACK-BACKED GULL
Larus fuscus L55cm
Characteristics: A large gull with slate grey wings and back and contrasting black wing tips. Birds from the far north have much blacker wings. Yellow legs in adults, but juveniles have pink legs until they moult into adult plumage. The bill is smaller than in the other large gulls but still has the orange spot on the lower mandible.

Habits and similar species: Like other gulls is an opportunist feeder and may visit refuse tips and fish quays as well as feeding along the shore line and on open sea. May also raid other birds' nests at breeding colonies. Great Black-back is much larger and darker, and Herring Gull is slightly larger with silver-grey wings.

25

Great black-backed gull

Distribution and habitat:
Breeds on rocky coasts and islands. Found with other nesting seabirds, but in winter may disperse wide-

ly, sometimes going inland to join other gulls. Often nests on promontories near, but not in, colonies of other gulls.

	JAN	FEB	MAR	APR	MAY	JUN	JULY	AUG	SEPT	OCT	NOV	DEC
PRESENT												
BREEDING												
SONG												

GREAT BLACK-BACKED GULL
Larus marinus L70cm
Characteristics: A very large gull with all black wings and back. Its massive yellow bill has an orange spot at the tip and its legs are flesh-coloured. The deep, angry-sounding 'kow kow' call can be heard above the clamour of other gulls. Often seen standing on an outcrop surveying the surrounding coastline.

Habits and similar species: Able to consume quite large prey such as nesting auks or rabbits, and the solitary nests are often littered with the bones of their prey. May be confused with the Scandinavian race of the Lesser Black-back, but it is much larger and lacks the yellow legs.

GLAUCOUS GULL
Larus hyperboreus L70cm
Characteristics: A very large gull, although some birds may be similar in size to the Herring Gull, with pale silvery wings and back and pink legs. The large bill has the typical orange spot at the tip. Juveniles are much paler than juveniles of other large gulls, and the buff coloured wings have very pale tips.

Distribution and habitat: A breeding bird in Iceland and Svalbard, nesting on rocky cliffs and rough stony shores. An unusual winter

visitor to the coastline of Britain, more often seen in northern regions where it may frequent fish quays with other gulls.

Habits and similar species: Feeds on a variety of foods which it finds by scavenging and following fishing boats; will take eggs and young of other seabirds. May be confused with Iceland Gull which is much smaller, with more slender bill and has more lively, buoyant flight.

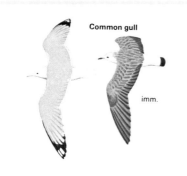

Common gull

imm.

COMMON GULL
Larus canus L41cm
Characteristics: A small gull, similar to the Herring Gull, but with greenish-yellow legs and a smaller yellowish bill lacking the red spot. In winter the white head is streaked with brownish marks. Call is a higher-pitched and quieter version of the Herring Gull's 'kee-ya' call and there is also a chuckling 'kak-kak-kak' call made when birds are in large migrating flocks.

Distribution and habitat: Breeds commonly on the coasts of northern Britain, Baltic and Scandinavia, with some inland col-

onies near large lakes. Migrates south and west for the winter, often feeding on farmland and near large lakes; is becoming common in urban situations.

Habits and similar species: May feed some distance from the sea, taking insects and soil invertebrates on farmland; also feeds at sea, usually in noisy flocks. May be confused with winter Black-headed Gull, but wings do not have trailing white edge and head lacks the black smudge. Rare Ring-billed Gull from N. America is larger (L48cm) and has dark ring around tip of bill.

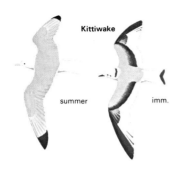

Kittiwake

summer   imm.

KITTIWAKE
Rissa tridactyla L41cm
Characteristics: A small sea-going gull with short black legs and webbed feet with claws which enable it to grip on narrow rock ledges on the breeding cliffs. Its grey wings have black tips with no white markings on them and there is no orange spot on the small yellow bill. Immature birds have a striking pattern of black and grey on the wings with a black bar at the end of the slightly forked tail and a black band across the back of the neck.

Distribution and habitat: Common, breeds on rocky coasts, nesting in large, noisy colonies on steep cliffs or waterside buildings. In winter they move south and disperse over the Atlantic, North Sea and western Mediterranean, often following fishing fleets.

Habits and similar species: Feed on the open sea on small surface-feeding fish and offal which they pick from the surface, making very shallow splashy dives. They make a far-carrying 'kitt-ee-wayke' call incessantly at the breeding colony. May be confused with the Common Gull; juveniles may be confused with adult Sabine's Gull which has black, white and grey pattern on wings but no black bar on tail or neck.

27

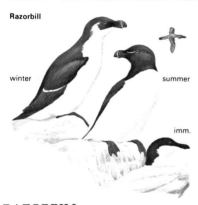

Razorbill

winter   summer

imm.

RAZORBILL
Alca torda L41cm
Characteristics: A compact black and white seabird with a flattened bill. Underside is white, upperparts are all black apart from a thin white wing-bar, a white line from the eye to the bill and a white stripe across the bill. In winter, cheeks and throat become white. At the breeding colonies a deep growling call can be heard. Flies with rapid whirring wing-beats and shows an up-turned tail when on the water.

Distribution and habitat: Breeds on rocky cliffs and islands, commoner to the north. Forms quite large colonies in suitable areas. Single egg laid on bare rock in a crevice or beneath a boulder. Some winter near the coast, but most are further out to sea.

Habits and similar species: Dives for fish from the surface, sometimes close to the shore, but often far out to sea. Swims well under water using wings like flippers. Susceptible to oil pollution; also killed in large numbers by fishing nets. At a distance may be confused with Guillemot, but is blacker with larger bill. Immatures may be confused with young Puffin, but face is black, not grey as in Puffin.

Puffin

summer   winter

imm.

Distribution and habitat:
Breeds in sometimes huge colonies on grassy cliffs and islands where burrows are excavated. Some nesting material is used and a single egg is laid. More numerous in far northern colonies, but there have been huge declines in some areas.

PUFFIN
Fratercula arctica L30cm

Characteristics: An unmistakable black and white seabird with a massive colourful bill. The face is white in the breeding season and the eyes are surrounded by a colourful eye-ring. The large red and yellow bill plates are shed in the winter and it is then smaller and less colourful. At the breeding colony Puffins make a comical 'arr arr arr' call, but at sea they are silent. They spend the winter far out to sea and little is known about their habits then.

Habits and similar species: Dives for fish, especially sand eels, and can carry several fish at once due to serrated edge of bill and tongue. At the breeding colony, large numbers may gather in the evenings outside their burrows, then suddenly disappear below ground. Colonies may appear to be deserted for a few days if feeding birds move far offshore for food. Winter birds may be confused with Razorbills.

28

Guillemot

winter

summer

GUILLEMOT
Uria aalge L42cm
Characteristics: A black and white sea-bird with a pointed bill. Southern races appear chocolate brown, moulting to a greyish colour in winter. A pale white wing bar is visible and some birds have a striking white eye-ring and facial stripe; more frequent in the north. Colonies can be very noisy.

Distribution and habitat: Guillemots breed on inaccessible cliffs on rocky coasts and islands and some colonies contain many thousands of birds. There is no nest and the single egg is laid on the bare rock. In winter most go far out to sea, occasionally inshore in bad weather.

	JAN	FEB	MAR	APR	MAY	JUN	JULY	AUG	SEPT	OCT	NOV	DEC
PRESENT												
BREEDING												
SONG												

Habits and similar species: Guillemots dive for fish from the surface, and they can swim well under water using their wings. On the nesting ledges they often sit upright. They are very susceptible to oil pollution at sea and large numbers are killed each year. Brunnich's Guillemot is only found in the far north. It is like the Guillemot apart from a darker head and a shorter, more solid bill with a white line.

29

Black guillemot

summer

winter

BLACK GUILLEMOT
Cepphus grylle L34cm
Characteristics: A small all black sea-bird with a prominent white wing patch and red legs and feet. In winter the black plumage becomes mottled with grey and white and the underside is very pale, but the white wing patch is still very obvious. The call is a series of thin whistling sounds, reminiscent of a squeaking hinge.

Distribution and habitat: A common bird around rocky coasts of northern Britain, Iceland and Scandinavia, breeding in small scattered colonies on rocky shores, usually near shallow water.

	JAN	FEB	MAR	APR	MAY	JUN	JULY	AUG	SEPT	OCT	NOV	DEC
PRESENT												
BREEDING												
SONG												

Habits and similar species: Dives in shallow water for fish. Nests in crevices and under large boulders, laying two eggs, unlike the other auks. Does not migrate out to sea in the winter, staying close to its shallow water feeding grounds; some birds may move south. Winter birds much paler than other auks, but at great distance may be confused with a small grebe such as Black-necked Grebe.

LITTLE AUK
Alle alle L20cm

Characteristics: The smallest auk, and the smallest diving seabird, all black above with white underparts and a faint white wing bar. The bill and the tail are very short. In winter the cheeks and the sides of the neck become white. Excited chattering calls are heard at the breeding colony, but no calls have been heard from birds at sea.

Distribution and habitat: Nests in huge colonies on Svalbard and Greenland with a few birds in northern Iceland. Prefers rocky cliffs with boulders and deep crevices offering safe nesting sites. Migrates as far south as northern Britain in winter, stragglers further south.

Habits and similar species: Dives for small crustaceans, often close to shore, but can feed at great distances from land, carrying food back to the colony in a distended crop. May be confused with very young Razorbill or Puffin, but bill is even smaller and tail is much shorter.

Rock dove

ROCK DOVE
Columba livia L33cm

Characteristics: The wild Rock Dove, at home on sea cliffs, is the ancestor of the Feral Pigeon, a familiar bird of towns and cities. In flight, two black wing bars and a triangular white rump patch are distinctive features. The 'coo-roo-coo' call is similar to Feral Pigeon's but difficult to hear near the sea.

Distribution and habitat: True Rock Doves are now restricted to Scotland, Ireland and Faroe, and prefer rocky coastlines where secure nest sites are available. They will move on to cultivated land to feed, and also search for seeds on cliff tops and along the strand line.

Habits and similar species: Small flocks of Rock Doves can be observed on rocky headlands and may occasionally be found feeding further inland. They form a major source of food for the Peregrine. Feral Pigeons are much more variable, often lacking the wing bars and white rump. In southern Britain Feral Pigeons have reverted to cliff nesting sites and can often cause confusion.

Chough

imm.

CHOUGH
Pyrrhocorax pyrrhocorax L40cm
Characteristics: An all-black member of the Crow family with a curved red bill and red legs. Its harsh, metallic-sounding 'cheeow' call is heard frequently, and a quieter 'chuf' call gives the bird its English name. In flight, Choughs show distinct 'fingers' at the ends of the wing, and they engage in exciting aerobatic displays using up-draughts from cliffs.

Distribution and habitat: Found on mountains and sea-cliffs in western Britain and Ireland. Sometimes small colonies are formed along rocky cliffs. In winter birds may congregate in small flocks in coastal feeding areas. Close-cropped grassland with a high ant population is favoured.

Habits and similar species: The long down-curved bill is used to probe into turf for small insects, especially ants, but it is also used to turn over seaweed in winter in search of sand-hoppers and kelp-flies. Juvenile Choughs have a more yellowish bill, similar to the shorter, bright yellow bill of the Alpine Chough. At a distance, may be confused with Jackdaw but has no grey.

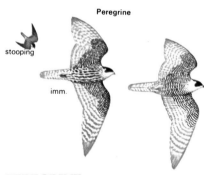

Peregrine

stooping

imm.

PEREGRINE
Falco peregrinus L40cm-46cm
Characteristics: A powerful falcon with a distinctive anchor-shaped outline in flight. The tail is short and the long wings are markedly pointed. Rapid wingbeats are often followed by long glides. When pursuing prey there is often a steep and powerful dive from a great height. Plumage varies from a dark to light grey above and light to buff colour below with dark barrings. There is always a pronounced moustachial stripe. Females much larger than males. Call a harsh 'kek-kek-kek-kek'.

Distribution and habitat: Widespread but rare on rocky coasts and mountainous regions. Some birds breed on tall buildings in towns. In winter may leave breeding areas and follow flocks of waders and wildfowl to estuaries and marshes.

Habits and similar species: Pursues quite large birds up to Rock Dove, Grouse and Mallard size. Nests on ledges on very steep cliffs, on sites which may have been used for centuries. Numbers building up after decline due to pesticide poisoning, but now prone to egg-collecting and chick-stealing by falconers.

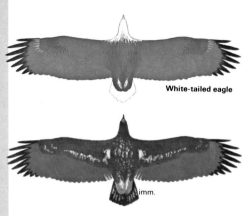

White-tailed eagle

imm.

WHITE-TAILED EAGLE
Haliaeetus albicilla L70-90cm
Characteristics: A massive bird of prey with a distinctive white tail. In flight the wings look very broad and show 'fingers' at the tips. The white tail is wedge shaped; in juveniles it is brown but still has the wedge shape, unlike the square tail of the Golden Eagle. Adults have pale, almost white heads. The flight is slow with deep wing-beats rather like a heron.

32

Distribution and habitat: A very scarce breeding bird, re-introduced into Britain, still present in Iceland and Scandinavia. Prefers remote rocky coastlines or large lakes. Nests on cliffs or in large trees, using huge quantities of twigs. Some birds migrate to lakes in winter.

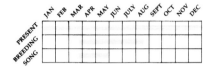

Habits and similar species: May scavenge for food, but will also catch fish or take large seabirds up to size of Glaucous Gull. Often flies low over water or reed beds. Similar to Golden Eagle, but is more vulture-like in behaviuor and wedge-shaped tail and only partially feathered legs are different.

Raven

RAVEN
Corvus corax L64cm
Characteristics: The largest all black member of the Crow family with a massive bill and a wedge-shaped tail. The black plumage has a deep gloss when seen in good light. Ravens engage in stunning aerobatics, including a deep twisting dive and upside-down flying. When walking Ravens have a strange rolling gait. The deep 'cronk' call is louder than that of any other crow.

Distribution and habitat: A widespread breeding bird on rocky coasts, mountains and heavily wooded country. Nests on cliffs and in trees, using twigs and then sheep's wool for a lining

Habits and similar species: Feeds on carrion, but also kills quite large prey such as rabbits and medium-sized birds. Will also feed on seeds, fruits and soil invertebrates. Usually remains near the breeding area for the winter, but may leave the highest mountain tops in very harsh weather. Carrion Crow is also all black, but has more slender bill and square-cut tail.

Shorelark

imm.

♂ summer

SHORELARK
Eremophila alpestris L16cm
Characteristics: A distinctive bird in summer plumage with bold black and yellow patterning on the head. At close range the male's small 'horns' are visible. In winter the head markings are far less distinct, but the underside is still white. The song is a muted version of the Skylark's and is usually delivered from the ground.

Distribution and habitat: Breeds in mountains and tundra in Scandinavia, but moves to sandy and shingle shores in eastern Britain and northern Europe in winter, often feeding in mixed flocks with Snow and Lapland Buntings.

Habits and similar species: Feeds on seeds and insects collected from the ground and often runs very fast rather than flies from any disturbance. Sometimes makes a pipit-like 'tsip' call. At a distance winter birds may look like an unstreaked Skylark, but facial markings separate it from other larks. Short-toed Lark is also unstreaked below but it has a much paler head.

33

ROCK PIPIT
Anthus spinoletta L17cm
Characteristics: A greyish-brown, dark-legged pipit with a long bill. An aerial song flight indicates their breeding area. Birds soar out from a low perch and then 'parachute' down giving rather flat trilling song.

Distribution and habitat: A widespread and sometimes common breeding bird around rocky coasts in Britain, northern Europe and southern Scandinavia. Usually nests in small rock crevices. May move to sandy shores to feed along strand lines in winter,

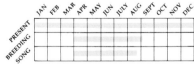

Habits and similar species: Feeds on insects and small seeds gathered from the ground among low vegetation and will also feed on marine invertebrates on the shore. The Water Pipit is a race of the Rock Pipit, not a separate species. It is greyer than the Rock Pipit and has white, not grey outer tail feathers. Water Pipits breed in mountains, migrating to lower altitudes to feed on marshes and meadows in the winter.

Snow bunting

SNOW BUNTING
Plectrophenax nivalis L16.5cm
Characteristics: In breeding season male is black and white with short black bill. Female has buff-brown upperparts and pale underside with black bill. Male is similar to females and juveniles in winter with yellow-orange bill. White wing patches and underparts are distinctive at all seasons. A gentle 'trrrp' and a short 'teu' call are heard throughout the year.

Distribution and habitat: Breeds in open stony habitats in mountains, and sometimes near sea-level in the far north of its range, moving to low lying areas for the winter. Often forms large mixed flocks along sandy shores and dunes in winter, feeding on seeds.

Habits and similar species: May be the only small songbird in many of its remote mountain habitats and the male's song carries some distance. The nest is usually concealed in a small rock crevice. Insects are taken in the summer, but the normal diet is small seeds. In breeding season male is much whiter than the Lapland Bunting, and in winter both sexes lack the brown coloration on the back.

Lapland bunting

LAPLAND BUNTING
Calcarius lapponicus L15cm
Characteristics: Breeding males have a black head and neck with a chestnut nape. The bill is yellow and there is a pale buff eye stripe. The upperparts are mottled brown with chestnut shoulder patches. Females are similar above, but lack the black head. Winter males lose most of the black coloration, looking more like females.

Distribution and habitat: Breeds on tundra and moorland in Scandinavia, but moves to coasts and lower moorland in winter. A regular passage migrant to Britain when it may form mixed flocks with other buntings and larks on sandy shores or heaths.

Habits and similar species: Females and winter males are very similar to Reed Bunting, but differ in having yellow bill and chestnut nape. Male Rustic Bunting has white throat and chestnut chest band in summer.

winter

imm.

Slavonian grebe

summer

SLAVONIAN GREBE
Podiceps auritus L33cm
Characteristics: A medium sized diving bird with black back, crown and cheeks and deep red flanks and neck. The 'horns' which give it its other name of 'Horned Grebe' are a rich yellow orange. In winter the neck and face are white, with the black head giving a 'capped' appearance. The black bill is straight with a pale tip. In flight the wings show white shoulders.

Distribution and habitat: A rare breeding bird in northern Britain; commoner in Iceland and Scandinavia. Usually nests

on small lakes with plenty of vegetation. In winter moves to the coast, estuaries or ice-free lakes, and may form small, loose groups with other grebes.

Habits and similar species: Entirely aquatic and quite unable to walk on land. Feeds on aquatic insects and crustaceans in summer, and mainly fish in winter. The largest and longest-necked of the small grebes, distinguished from Black-necked by straight, not upwards pointing bill, and from Red-necked by pale tip to bill, not yellow base.

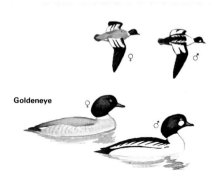

Goldeneye

GOLDENEYE
Bucephala clangula L46cm
Characteristics: A diving duck with a markedly peaked head, almost triangular in shape. Drakes have a glossy green head with a bright yellow eye and small white cheek patch, but ducks have a brown head without the cheek patch. Both sexes show a broad white wing bar in flight. In the breeding season males make a rather nasal 'speer speer' call and females make a more typical duck-like 'kurr kurr' sound.

Distribution and habitat: A rare breeding bird in Scotland, becoming much more common in Scandinavia, nesting in

holes or hollow trees beside lakes in wooded areas; can take to nest boxes. In winter they move to the coast and large freshwater lakes and reservoirs.

Habits and similar species: Goldeneyes dive frequently for their food which they find on the bottom of sometimes quite deep lakes, estuaries or coastal bays. A wide range of aquatic invertebrates, including insect larvae, crustaceans and molluscs, but rarely take fish. Barrow's Goldeneye is restricted to Iceland and has a glossy purple head with a larger white crescent-shaped white spot on the cheek.

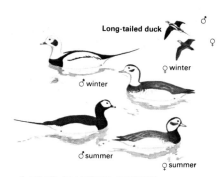

Long-tailed duck

♂ winter

♀ winter

♂ summer

♀ summer

LONG-TAILED DUCK
Clangula hyemalis L41-53cm
Characteristics: The drake is a striking black and white diving duck with a very long pointed tail. In summer the male is mostly black on the face, neck and breast, with a brown back and white cheeks; females are paler on the neck and face. In winter males have a mainly white head and neck, and females look browner on the back. The females lack the long tail. The male's strange yodelling calls are heard on the breeding grounds; females sound more duck-like.

Distribution and habitat: Nests are built beside coastal or freshwater pools in Arctic tundra in Iceland, Greenland and Scandinavia.

In winter most birds move to the coast, although not many of them stray far from their breeding area. A few wander as far south as southern Britain.

Habits and similar species: Small crustaceans and molluscs are collected from the bottom by making rapid dives. In summer a large number of insects, particularly blackfly larvae, are taken from freshwater. Short bill and very long tail distinguish Long-tailed Drake from drake Smew. Duck's face pattern more distinctive than darker face of female Common and Velvet Scoters.

Red-breasted merganser

RED-BREASTED MERGANSER
Mergus serrator L55cm
Characteristics: Large diving duck with long, narrow bill. The hooked tip and serrated edge are unlike any other, apart from Goosander and Smew. Both sexes have an untidy crest, but colours are different: ducks have rusty brown head, drakes glossy green with a bold white collar. In flight, drakes show a broad white wing patch, but ducks have a smaller trailing white patch.

Distribution and habitat: A widespread breeding bird in northern Britain, Iceland and Scandinavia, nesting in dense

vegetation or rock crevices beside lakes and rivers. In winter most birds move to the coast and estuaries, some going as far south as the Mediterranean.

Habits and similar species: Mergansers are experts at chasing and catching fish underwater, and the serrated bill helps them to hold on to fish as slippery as eels, but they may sometimes also take other prey such as large shrimps. The Goosander is larger and has a white breast and flanks tinged with pink. Duck Goosander is larger and greyer above with more down-turned crest.

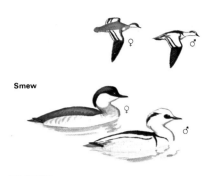

Smew

Distribution and habitat:
Breeds on freshwater lakes, often with wooded margins, in far northern Scandinavia and northern Europe. Winters on lowland reservoirs, lakes, sheltered coastal bays and estuaries, mainly in south-east England and north-west Europe.

	JAN	FEB	MAR	APR	MAY	JUN	JULY	AUG	SEPT	OCT	NOV	DEC
PRESENT												
BREEDING												
SONG												

SMEW
Mergus albellus L41cm
Characteristics: Drake is a small, boldly marked, black and white diving duck with a serrated-edged, dark bill, mostly white head and black eye patches. The duck is greyer with a chestnut cap and white pattern of bars in flight, unlike large white patches of Goldeneye. The calls are not often heard, but consist of quiet whistles and 'kurr-ick' sounds. Drake's display involves raising crest and drawing back head. Sometimes found with Goldeneye and has hybridised.

Habits and similar species: Feeds mostly on small fish caught by diving from the surface; also takes aquatic insect larvae on summer breeding lakes. Nests in tree holes, using female down feathers for lining. Female Merganser and Goosander are larger than female Smew, with more chestnut on head and no white cheeks. Drake Goosander is larger than drake Smew, with dark glossy head and slender red bill.

37

Shelduck

Distribution and habitat:
Common, breeds on most coasts with intertidal mud and sand. Nests concealed in rabbit burrows or beneath bushes. In winter many birds move to large muddy estuaries; a huge concentration builds up at the River Elbe mouth to moult before dispersing.

	JAN	FEB	MAR	APR	MAY	JUN	JULY	AUG	SEPT	OCT	NOV	DEC
PRESENT												
BREEDING												
SONG												

SHELDUCK
Tadorna tadorna L61cm
Characteristics: A large duck with a glossy green head and bright red bill. The body is mostly white, but there is a chestnut chest-band and a black stripe along the wings. The sexes are identical apart from a large lump on top of the bill which the drake develops in summer. In flight the drake can be heard to make a series of whistling calls, sounding rather like wingbeats, and the ducks make a laughing 'ak ak ak ak'.

Habits and similar species: The broad bill is used to sieve through intertidal mud and sand for small invertebrates, principally the tiny mollusc, *Hydrobia*. The Ruddy Shelduck has deep reddish-brown plumage and a smaller dark bill. The Egyptian Goose, introduced from Africa, is buff-brown or greyish with a pink bill and feeds on plant material.

dark-breasted
light-breasted
Brent goose

BRENT GOOSE
Branta bernicla L58cm
Characteristics: A small, compact goose, smaller than a Shelduck, with an all-black head and black legs and feet. The black neck has white patches at the side, which are absent in juveniles. In flight the black tail shows a V-shaped white bar. The call is a hoarse 'grruk grruk grruk' and is frequently heard in feeding and flying flocks in winter. Pale-breasted birds come from Greenland and Svalbard, but dark-breasted birds are from Arctic Europe and Asia.

38

Distribution and habitat: Breeds on tundra, usually near the sea, in the Arctic, migrating south to coasts of southern Britain and Ireland and north-west Europe for the winter. Prefers estuaries and salt-marshes but will also feed on coastal farmland.

Habits and similar species: Grazes on grasses and green algae, but prefers Eel-grass. Will take growing crops on coastal farmland. Barnacle Goose has paler breast, greyer back, white face. Canada Goose much larger, browner back and white chin. Red-breasted Goose rare vagrant from Asia and extreme E. Europe. All black apart from chestnut breast and neck, white stripes on sides of neck and below wings.

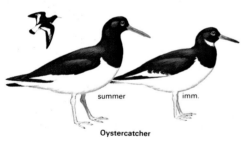
summer
imm.
Oystercatcher

OYSTERCATCHER
Haematopus ostralegus L43cm
Characteristics: A large wader with black and white plumage, a long orange bill and pink legs. In summer the throat is all black, but in winter it shows a white patch. The broad white wing bar shows well in flight. Juveniles are browner with a shorter bill. The usual call is a far-carrying, shrill 'kleeep', but there are many shorter 'pic pic' sounds heard when threatened by predators or when squabbling. A loud, piping display call is made communally by birds running around with their bills pointing downwards.

Distribution and habitat: A widespread and sometimes common breeding bird on all coasts, and sometimes inland on rough farmland and stony river beds. Some birds migrate from more northerly breeding grounds but most stay close to the coast.

Habits and similar species: The powerful bill can be used to tackle quite tough prey like limpets and crabs, but is also used to probe mud for invertebrates. The nest is a shallow depression with little lining material, often close to water, but sometimes in vegetation. No other large, long-billed wader has an all black back and white underside.

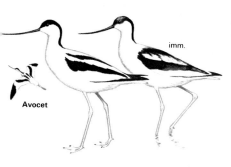

Avocet

imm.

AVOCET
Recurvirostra avosetta L43cm

Characteristics: A striking black-and-white wader with long blue-grey legs and a strongly up-curved bill. The call is a melodious 'kluit' but there is also a yelping cry given when intruders stray too close to the nest. Juveniles show more brown coloration on the wings and back. When feeding in deep water the long legs may not be so obvious and the bill may be hidden, but the side-to-side sweeping motion of the head is characteristic.

Distribution and habitat: A local breeding bird on brackish and salt-water marshes near the sea, some-times further in-land, mainly in south-east Britain and the N European and Baltic coasts. In winter many birds migrate south and west, congregating in large flocks.

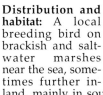

Habits and similar species: The up-curved bill is used to sieve through water or fine mud for small invertebrates. The nest is built in a small hollow in dried-up mudflats and sometimes on low islands, usually in small colonies. The Black-winged Stilt has a straight finely--pointed bill, and all black back and wings with very long bright-red legs.

39

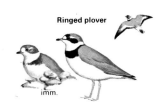

Ringed plover

imm.

RINGED PLOVER
Charadrius hiaticula L19cm

Characteristics: A medium-sized wading bird with a short bill and a distinctive black-and-white head and neck pattern. The short orange bill has a black tip and the legs are orange-yellow. In flight the wings show a pale wing bar and trailing black edge. In winter the black markings fade to brown; juveniles also have brown, not black markings on the head and an incomplete neck band. The fluty di-syllabic call is given during a fluttering display flight, but there are many other quieter notes given from the ground.

Distribution and habitat: A widespread, sometimes common bird on shingle or sandy shores, and some-times on low rocky islands or stony river beds. In winter birds from the north migrate to southern estuaries and mudflats, often forming mixed flocks with other waders.

Habits and similar species: A characteristic method of feeding is to run a short distance and then pause as if listening before stabbing at a small prey item, usually a tiny worm; many small invertebrates are taken, the species depending on the type of habitat. The Little Ringed Plover is smaller with yellow eye ring and no wing bar. The Kentish Plover is also smaller and much paler with no black neck band.

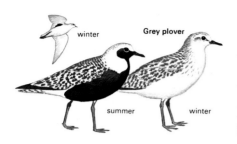

GREY PLOVER
Pluvialis squatarola L28cm
Characteristics: A plump, medium-sized wader, distinguished in all plumages by striking black axillaries (arm-pits) and a whitish rump, both seen well in flight. In summer the face, neck and breast are black, bordered by white, and the upperparts are mottled grey. In winter the underside is more uniform grey and there is a pale white stripe over the eye. Juveniles are brownish, rather than grey on their backs. The three-note 'tee-oo-ee' call sounds like a person whistling.

40

Distribution and habitat: Breeds on coastal tundra in European Arctic, but migrates south to western Europe and the Mediterranean for the winter. Some linger on wintering grounds for much of the year. Prefers estuaries and muddy seashores; an unusual bird inland.

Habits and similar species: Found on mudflats with other waders but rarely in large numbers or close concentrations. Feeds on marine worms hunted by sight, but will also take small crustaceans and molluscs. The Golden Plover has white axillaries and rich yellow-brown upperparts. The rare Lesser Golden Plover has grey axillaries, and is slightly smaller and slimmer.

TURNSTONE
Arenaria interpres L23cm
Characteristics: A medium-sized compact wader with short orange legs and a short, but powerful bill. In flight the wings show a striking black and white pattern. Breeding plumage is a mixture of rich orange-brown, especially on the back, and black and white on the chest and wings. A variety of short twittering call notes are made, especially if a flock of birds is disturbed when feeding; sometimes a bird perched on a rock will alert many other waders with this call.

Distribution and habitat: Common on rocky and weed-covered shores, and may mingle with small flocks of Purple Sandpipers. Sometimes found on open mudflats. Breeds on coasts of Baltic, Scandinavia and Arctic Europe, may very rarely breed in northern Britain.

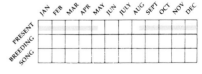

Habits and similar species: The short bill is used to turn over small stones and seaweed in search of food. It is also used to open shells of small crabs and molluscs and sometimes probe mud for marine worms. In summer on the breeding grounds the main prey is insects. Winter Dotterel has longer yellow legs and no black on the chest, and is not likely to turn up on stony shores.

CURLEW SANDPIPER
Calidris ferruginea L19cm
Characteristics: An uncommon wader, seen mainly on its autumn migration. Its down-curved bill and white rump, seen clearly in flight distinguish it from other small waders. In breeding plumage it has rich reddish-brown underparts, but is greyer on the back and white under the tail. Winter plumage is a much paler grey with all white underparts. Juveniles have a pale orange-buff coloration on the sides of the neck.

Distribution and habitat: A breeding bird of the Siberian arctic tundra, moving to coasts for winter, preferring muddy shores and saltmarshes. Most birds make for North Africa and the Red Sea, but some are seen in early autumn whilst on passage, often with Dunlin.

Habits and similar species: The down-curved bill is used to probe soft mud for invertebrates which are usually caught in very shallow water. In summer on the tundra insects form the main part of the diet. The Dunlin is slightly smaller with shorter legs and does not have such a long down-curved bill. Green and Wood Sandpipers also have white rumps, but they have much shorter straight bills.

41

DUNLIN
Calidris alpina L18cm
Characteristics: A common, but, variable, small wader with black legs and bill. In summer adults have brown upperparts and a black belly, but in winter they are grey above and white below. Juveniles show heavily spotted flanks and grey-brown upperparts. On migration Dunlin fly in tight flocks and engage in many twists and turns with the flock appearing to change colour from white to grey. The nasal 'zee' call is sometimes repeated rapidly many times and sound like a trill.

Distribution and habitat: A widespread breeding bird of upland habitats in Britain and more coastal areas in the Arctic. Nests concealed in grass tussocks or heather. In winter there is a large migration south to estuaries and mudflats, with many arriving in Britain.

Habits and similar species: Feed in large flocks on small invertebrates of intertidal mud, and roost on shingle banks and dunes at high tide. Races from different breeding grounds vary slightly in size, bill length and curvature and winter colour. Sanderling look much paler in winter and have a shorter bill. Stints are smaller still, with very short bills. Winter Knot is larger and lacks white sides to rump.

Distribution and habitat: A breeding bird in the Arctic tundra and on northern coastal marshes. A few birds are regular passage migrants in Britain and northern Europe, turning up on coastal marshes and shallow pools, usually with other small waders.

LITTLE STINT
Calidris minuta L13cm

Characteristics: A very small wader with short legs and a short, straight bill. In summer the back and wings are brown with distinct V-marks on them; in winter they are greyer, but the V-marks can still just be detected. In flight there is a distinct white wing bar, and the sides of the rump are white. The underside is mostly white in winter. Sometimes a short 'tic' flight call is heard, especially if the bird is alarmed.

Habits and similar species: The short bill is used to collect tiny invertebrates from the surface of mudflats and brackish pools; in summer terrestrial insects are the main food available. Temminck's Stint is very similar, but the short bill is slightly down-curved and the outer tail feathers are white. When alarmed, Temminck's Stint is more likely to rise up rapidly making a spluttering alarm call.

Distribution and habitat: In summer confined to Arctic tundra in Greenland and Siberia. Nests on ground in low vegetation. May appear briefly inland on passage; normally move to European and Mediterranean coast. In winter flocks gather on sandy and muddy shores.

KNOT
Calidris canutus L25cm

Characteristics: A medium-sized, plump wader, with a short but stout bill, and greenish legs. Plumage mostly grey in winter with a pale underside. A pale wing bar can be seen in flight, and there is a trailing black edge to the wing. The tail is grey, showing no dark edges or rump patch. In summer the underside is more rufous and the upperparts are darker reddish-brown. The 'knut knut' call is quiet and hard to hear above the calls of other waders.

Habits and similar species: Flocks often feed together with heads all pointing down at same time. Usual diet consists of small intertidal invertebrates, but in summer more insects are taken. Dunlin is much smaller with slightly down-curved bill and dark centre to white rump. Sanderling is paler with very short bill and is more active. Grey Plover larger, more solitary, has shorter bill, black axillaries.

summer

Sanderling

winter

winter

SANDERLING
Calidris alba L20cm
Characteristics: A small wader with bright grey and white plumage, a small black bill and short black legs. Its habit of running up and down sandy shores at the edge of the waves, just avoiding getting soaked distinguish it from other small waders. In the breeding season the head and breast are more rufous. A white wing bar with a trailing black edge and a white rump with a black centre and black tail are distinctive in flight.

Distribution and habitat: Breeds on Arctic tundra in Greenland, migrating south for the winter. Some winter along British coasts, others are only passage migrants, continuing south to Africa. Prefers open sandy beaches in winter where food is caught at the shoreline.

	JAN	FEB	MAR	APR	MAY	JUN	JULY	AUG	SEPT	OCT	NOV	DEC
PRESENT												
BREEDING												
SONG												

Habits and similar species: A very active bird, running rather than walking after its prey and more likely to run from danger than fly. If disturbed may fly off for short distance and then return to same spot to continue feeding. Sometimes roosts on rocks at edge of sandy beaches. Much paler than Dunlin with more marked wing bar. Smaller than Knot, with darker legs and more white on tail.

winter

winter

summer   Purple sandpiper

PURPLE SANDPIPER
Calidris maritima L21cm
Characteristics: A medium-sized compact wader with a solid down-curved bill and yellow legs. From a distance and in flight looks very dark, paler underneath with spotted flanks. Summer adults and juveniles are paler and more speckled, and in very good light a slight purple gloss may be detected in breeding adults. A pale white wing bar is visible in flight; the white rump has a dark central line. When disturbed a quiet 'tweet-wit' call is given, sometimes repeated as a trilling call.

Distribution and habitat: A very rare breeding bird in Scotland, found mainly in Iceland and Scandinavia. A few birds linger around the coast for most of the year. Nests on the ground in low vegetation. In winter moves to rocky and weedy seashores; also on breakwaters.

	JAN	FEB	MAR	APR	MAY	JUN	JULY	AUG	SEPT	OCT	NOV	DEC
PRESENT												
BREEDING												
SONG												

Habits and similar species: Often very confiding, and frequently associated with Turnstones. May roost very close to the water in small groups. Feeds on invertebrates picked from the rocks; eats mainly insects in the summer. Curlew Sandpiper slightly smaller and slimmer, paler in colour with more pronounced down-curved bill. Dunlin smaller, paler with shorter less stocky bill and less likely to feed on rocks.

Grey phalarope

imm.

imm.

♀ summer

GREY PHALAROPE
Phalaropus fulicarius L20cm

Characteristics: A small wader usually seen swimming. The short stout bill is yellow at the base, and the feet are lobed. Usually seen in winter when plumage is uniform grey above and white below. The wings show a white wing bar and trailing black edge in flight. In summer the underside is a rich red and the upperparts are browner with the face still white.

Distribution and habitat: A rare breeding bird in Iceland and more northerly areas, usually seen on passage in the autumn, especially after storms. Breeds beside shallow pools near the coast. Often feeds in similar places when storm-driven; usually winters at sea.

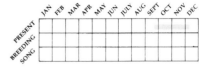

Habits and similar species: A buoyant swimmer, collecting small food items from the surface, sometimes swimming in circles, sometimes more erratically. Usually very confiding. Rather weak and fluttering flight, usually low over the water. Red-necked Phalarope is slightly smaller and has more pointed, all-dark bill. Wings look much darker in flight, and only neck is red in breeding season.

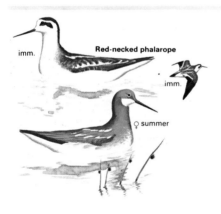

imm.

Red-necked phalarope

imm.

♀ summer

RED-NECKED PHALAROPE
Phalaropus lobatus L18cm

Characteristics: A scarce wader much more likely to be seen on water than on land. In summer the neck and sides of the throat are orange red. Females have a grey nape and males, which have a duller red throat, have a browner nape. Juveniles have an all white throat. In winter the upperparts are a slightly speckled grey and the underside is white.

Distribution and habitat: A scarce and declining breeding bird in Scotland, commoner in Iceland and Scandinavia. Nests close to water beneath overhanging grasses. Prefers small freshwater pools, sometimes inland in summer, but in winter may feed far out to sea.

Habits and similar species: Often a very confiding bird. Swims on shallow pools in pursuit of aquatic insects, picking them delicately from the surface. Females indulge in a courtship display, leaving the more subdued-coloured male to do the incubating. Wilson's Phalarope, a rare vagrant from N. America is larger (L23cm) with longer legs and a longer bill and is more likely to be seen running on land.

45

Redshank

REDSHANK
Tringa totanus L28cm

Characteristics: A long-legged, long-billed wader with grey-brown plumage; uniformly grey in winter, browner in summer. In flight the bold white hind-wing and white rump contrast with dark upperparts. The orange bill and legs show well in good light. A very vocal bird; the loud yelping 'tyu-yu-yu' calls are far-carrying; a trilling, melodious song is given from the ground or a post with wings raised.

Distribution and habitat: Common breeding wader of wet meadows, moorland or salt-marshes. Nests beneath grassy tussocks. In winter more likely to be seen on coast feeding on mudflats and open shores. Will take a range of invertebrates, especially marine worms.

Habits and similar species: Not usually found in large flocks, except at high tide roosts; more usually spread out over shore, sometimes bobbing head up and down if worried about an intruder. Spotted Redshank has no bar on wings and is much greyer. Greenshank is slightly larger and has greenish-yellow legs and slightly up-turned bill. Marsh Sandpiper is smaller, has dark legs and finer dark bill.

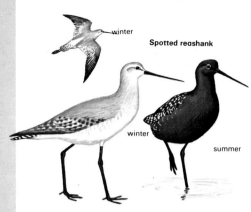

winter
Spotted reashank
winter
summer

SPOTTED REDSHANK
Tringa erythropus L30cm
Characteristics: An almost black wader in summer plumage with white speckling on the wings and back. Much paler in winter with white underparts. Legs dark red; long, slender bill red at base with hint of a down-turned tip. No wing bar seen in flight but wedge-shaped white rump and barred tail conspicuous. Usual call is a penetrating 'kloo-eet' or 'too-it'.

Distribution and habitat: Breeds on tundra, swampy ground and open forests in northern Scandinavia and Russia. Migrates

overland to coasts of southern Britain, western Europe and the Mediterranean for the winter, preferring brackish pools and sheltered estuaries.

Habits and similar species: Feeds more energetically than Redshank with a more stabbing action to the bill; often wades out into quite deep water and may even swim. Redshank shows white wing-band in flight and has shorter bill and Greenshank has more pronounced white rump with barring only at sides of tail. Ruff has much shorter bill and buff coloration in winter.

summer
Greenshank

GREENSHANK
Tringa nebularia L31cm
Characteristics: A slim wader with long olive-green legs and a slightly up-turned grey-blue bill. Grey plumage in winter with paler underside; head and neck paler than back and wings. A bold white rump patch, seen clearly in flight, extends as narrow white line up the back. Tail shows barring at sides only; no wing bar. Summer plumage slightly darker. The clear, fluty 'ru-tu' call is heard over the breeding grounds also a more shrill 'chu-chu-chu' call.

Distribution and habitat: A scarce breeding bird of wet moorlands and heaths in Scotland, but commoner in Scandinavia and

northern Europe. Nests are concealed in low vegetation. In winter they move to southern and western coasts, sometimes congregating in small groups.

Habits and similar species: Often runs after small fish in shallow water, but will also take range of small invertebrates caught in soft mud. Larger than Redshank and Spotted Redshank and usually more solitary. Rare transatlantic vagrants Lesser and Greater Yellowlegs both have bright yellow legs and darker brownish upperparts. Marsh Sandpiper is much smaller with thinner bill.

Ruff

♂winter

♂summer

RUFF
Philomachus pugnax L29-30cm
Characteristics: The male is unmistakable in summer with a striking neck frill and large ear tufts, ranging in colour from black, through speckled grey to brown. Females are smaller and more uniform in colour, being buff with dark-brown diamond-shaped specklings above and paler below. In winter both sexes are buff coloured.

Distribution and habitat: A rare breeding bird in Britain on freshwater marshes and swamps, becoming commoner in  northern Europe and Scandinavia. In winter is more likely to be seen on coastal marshes and wet fields near the sea, but may use wetlands inland.

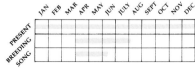

	JAN	FEB	MAR	APR	MAY	JUN	JULY	AUG	SEPT	OCT	NOV	DEC
PRESENT												
BREEDING												
SONG												

Habits and similar species: Males engage in an elaborate communal display at traditional 'lek' sites. Fierce attacks followed by deep bows are watched by females. May sometimes make a quiet grunting call. Flocks of both sexes look like two different species, and juveniles sometimes get confused with rare transatlantic waders. Head looks small in proportion to body and bill has very slightly down-turned tip.

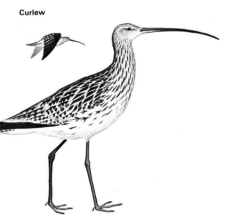

Curlew

CURLEW
Numenius arquata L55cm
Characteristics: A large wader with long legs and a very long down-curved bill. The upperparts are mottled brown and there is a bold white rump visible in flight. The tail shows dark barring on a brown background; primaries look darker than the rest of the wing. Calls include a liquid 'coor-lee' and a melodious bubbling call.

Distribution and habitat: A common and widespread breeding bird over much of Britain and northern Europe, nest- ing on moorland, marshes and wet meadows. Moves to coasts in winter, feeding on estuaries and saltmarshes; also occurs on grassy habitats.

	JAN	FEB	MAR	APR	MAY	JUN	JULY	AUG	SEPT	OCT	NOV	DEC
PRESENT												
BREEDING												
SONG												

Habits and similar species: Often feeds at the edge of the advancing tide on mudflats, probing deep into the mud for large marine worms; will also take small crustaceans and molluscs. Whimbrel is smaller with shorter bill and more pronounced dark and pale stripes on head. At great distance, and when feeding with heads down. Godwits may look similar, but both species have upwards-tilted bills.

Whimbrel

WHIMBREL
Numenius phaeopus L41cm

Characteristics: Noticeably smaller than the Curlew with a smaller down-curved bill. The wing-beats are more rapid and the call is a quieter seven-note trill, although there are some yelping calls reminiscent of Curlew. The pale buff and brown head markings show well at close range.

Distribution and habitat: A scarce breeding bird in northern Britain, more widespread and abundant in Iceland and Scandinavia. Nests on wet moorland and tundra, moving to coasts in winter. Occurs mainly as a passage migrant in Britain in spring and autumn.

Habits and similar species: Small excited flocks of Whimbrel are often seen migrating in the spring, stopping for a few days on estuaries and sandy shores, usually keeping separate from other waders. More solitary on the breeding grounds. Curlew is larger with longer bill and Godwits are similar sized but much more rufous in summer and greyer in winter with upturned bill.

Black-tailed godwit

winter

BLACK-TAILED GODWIT
Limosa limosa L41cm

Characteristics: A large wader with a bold black-and-white wing pattern and a striking black-and-white tail; in flight it looks similar to an Oystercatcher. A harsh 'wicka-wicka-wicka' call is heard in flight and a more lapwing-like 'pee-wit' call is also made near the breeding site. Less likely to indulge in aerial displays than the Bar-tailed Godwit.

Distribution and habitat: A rare breeding bird in southern Britain on damp meadows and marshes, more common on low-lying land in Europe. Moves south and west to the coast in winter, feeding on muddy shores, sometimes flying to grassland to roost at high tide.

Habits and similar species: A nervous and sometimes noisy bird feeding in small groups along the water's edge, flying off to roost before high tide. Tail and wing markings separate Black-tailed and Bar-tailed Godwits, and straighter, up-turned bill separate Godwits from Curlew and Whimbrel. Much larger than other common waders like Redshank and Greenshank.

winter

Bar-tailed godwit

summer

BAR-TAILED GODWIT
Limosa lapponica L38cm
Characteristics: A large wader with long legs and a long slightly up-turned bill. In summer underside is a rich reddish-brown and upperparts are mottled brown. Underside becomes very pale grey in winter. Tail shows distinct barring in flight and there is a small white rump patch but no wing bar.

Distribution and habitat: Breeds in the far north of Scandinavia and Europe on marshy, wetter areas of the tundra, migrating south and west for the winter. Occurs in Britain as a passage migrant and overwintering visitor to muddy shores and estuaries.

Habits and similar species: Flocks of Godwits sometimes perform aerobatics over their winter feeding grounds or roosts. They prefer to feed at the water's edge on a rising tide where they can catch marine worms and small crustaceans. At high tide they roost in large flocks, often with other waders. Black-tailed Godwit has white wing-bar and black and white, not barred, tail.

49

LITTLE GULL
Larus minutus L28cm
Characteristics: The smallest European gull. In summer the head is black down to the back of the neck. The wings have no black tips but are very dark grey below, with a trailing white edge and have a more rounded appearance than in the Black-headed Gull. The bill and legs are short and dark red. In winter the head is mostly white with a dark smudge behind the eye. The graceful, buoyant flight is similar to some species of marsh terns.

Distribution and habitat: A very occasional breeding bird in Britain, much more common on marshes on north European coast and inland in northern Europe. Nests by freshwater pools and marshy areas, moving to the coast in winter, but not often in very large numbers.

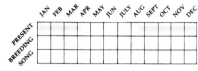

Habits and similar species: Hunts insects over freshwater in summer, taking them in the air and from the surface. In winter may feed with Black-headed Gulls near outfalls and on the shore. Lack of black on the wing-tips separates this from Black-headed. Mediterranean Gull also lacks black tips but is much larger (39cm) with larger red bill. Kittiwake has black wingtips and yellow bill.

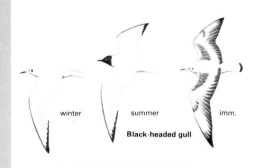

winter summer imm.

Black-headed gull

BLACK-HEADED GULL
Larus ridibundus L36cm
Characteristics: A medium-sized gull with a dark chocolate-brown hood in summer and a red bill and legs. In summer the hood does not extend as far as the nape; in winter it is reduced to dark smudges behind the eyes. The upperwings show large triangular white panels at the tips in flight and the underwings are grey, looking darker towards the tips. Juveniles are mottled brown on the wings and back with a black terminal tail band. First summer birds have brown primaries, but a greyer mantle with a dark tail band.

Distribution and habitat: A common breeding bird on freshwater and brackish marshes over a wide area of Britain and Europe.

Sometimes nests in colonies of several thousand pairs. In winter disperses over a wide range of marine and inland habitats from towns to farmland.

Habits and similar species: A noisy and gregarious gull feeding on flying insects, sometimes in marshes and reedbeds, and also taking a wide variety of other foods. May follow the plough with Common Gulls or scavenge on refuse tips with Herring Gulls. Mediterranean Gull is slightly larger, has more complete black, not brown, hood, and larger red bill. Common Gull has yellow-green legs and bill.

MEDITERRANEAN GULL
Larus melanocephalus L39cm
Characteristics: A medium-sized gull with a black hood in summer extending down to the nape. The wings are pale grey with a trailing white edge and there is no black at the tips. The large red bill has a dark band across the tip which appears to be slightly drooping. In winter the back of the head is smudged with black. Its usual call is a harsh 'kraar' which contrasts with the higher calls of Black-headed Gulls with which it sometimes nests.

Distribution and habitat: A very rare breeding bird in Britain, sometimes hybridising with Black-headed Gull. Mainly confined to low-lying lakes and coastal marshes in south-east Europe. Spreading north and west, and increasingly seen on passage and in winter.

Habits and similar species: Feeds on invertebrates and fish in shallow water also scavenges, joining flocks of other gulls, but may join other species in inland roosts in winter. Black-headed is smaller with smaller dark-brown hood. Little Gull has similar colourings but is much smaller. Transatlantic vagrant Bonaparte's Gull has smaller black bill and thin black borders to wings.

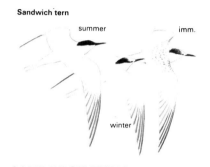

Sandwich tern

summer   imm.

winter

SANDWICH TERN
Sterna sandvicensis L41cm
Characteristics: A large, slim tern with a striking crested black head, short black legs and long yellow-tipped black bill. The mantle and wings are grey with no black tips and the underside is pure white. The tail is shorter than the wings when folded and quite deeply forked. The voice is a grating 'kirrick' or a more drawn-out 'kirr-whit' and is frequently heard when adults are bringing food to their young. The flight is powerful with rapid, deep wingbeats.

Distribution and habitat: A common summer visitor to sandy and shingly islands around Britain and northern Europe. Winters in Africa and eastern Mediterranean. Fishes further out to sea than other terns, often in quite rough water, and is far less likely to be seen inland.

Habits and similar species: Often the first of the terns to arrive in the spring, announcing its presence by its harsh calls. Dives powerfully for sand-eels and similar-sized fish. Fledged young sit waiting for adults to bring food which can be seen hanging from bill. Common and Arctic Terns are smaller with red bill and legs. Little Tern much smaller with yellow legs. Caspian Tern much larger with massive red bill.

51

ommon tern

summer   winter   imm.

COMMON TERN
Sterna hirundo L35cm
Characteristics: A medium-sized tern with black cap, red legs and black-tipped orange-red bill. Very similar to Arctic Tern but underside whiter and wings darker, especially at tips of the primaries, and less transparent in flight. The bill and legs also slightly longer. In flight, the forked tail shows shorter streamers and wing beats slower. Juveniles show a grey-brown scalloped pattern on the wings and a partly black head. Cry is a harsh, jarring 'kirri-kirri-kirri' with variations, and a screaming 'kree-ah' when intruders, especially humans, approach the nest too closely.

Distribution and habitat: Widespread, sometimes common in many coastal and freshwater sites. Nests on shingle beaches, specially constructed islands or inland lakes far from the sea; prefers sandy and shingly shores with shallow water for fishing. Migrates to African coast.

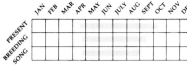

Habits and similar species: Dives for fish from the air, often hovering on buoyant wings. Nests in noisy colonies, sometimes with other terns. Very much like the Arctic Tern. Roseate Tern has all dark bill with red base, longer tail streamers and hint of pink on breast for short time in summer. Little Tern is smaller with yellow legs and black-tipped yellow bill.

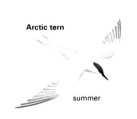

Arctic tern

summer

ARCTIC TERN
Sterna paradisaea L35cm
Characteristics: A medium-sized tern with a black cap, a coral-red bill and very short coral-red legs. Very similar to Common Tern especially at a distance; however, tail streamers are longer and wings are narrower with transparent appearance in the flight feathers. At closer range the underside is greyer, but the face is white giving the appearance of a white streak below the black cap. The legs are so short that sometimes the bird seems to be sitting. Voice can be harsher with a grating, staccato 'kt-kt-kt-kt' call and an angry-sounding 'kree-ah' call to warn off intruders straying too close to the nest.

Distribution and habitat: A common breeding bird of sandy and shingly shores, and rocky islands, usually more northerly than the Common Tern, although they often nest in mixed colonies. May nest far inland in northerly areas. Migrates to far southern latitudes for the winter.

Habits and similar species: Dives for fish from the air, but will also take small crustaceans and insects, sometimes from the surface of the water, and will pursue insects in flight. Very similar to Common Tern, but note shorter and brighter red legs and bill, more transparent wings, longer tail, greyer underside and different call.

ROSEATE TERN
Sterna dougallii L38cm
Characteristics: A medium-sized tern with black cap and black bill with barely-visible red base. In breeding season there is a pink flush to the underside (not an easily-spotted feature). The upperwings are very light grey so it looks much paler than Common Tern; tail streamers much longer.

Distribution and habitat: A scarce breeding bird in a few scattered localities around the coasts of Britain and extreme west- ern Europe. Usually nests colonially; mixes with Common and Arctic Terns. Migrates to west African coast for the winter where it is much persecuted.

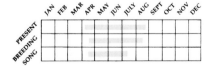

Habits and similar species: Even when fishing with other terns can be picked out by much whiter coloration and deeper 'zraaach' call. Almost exclusively marine, rarely turning up on freshwater. Sandwich Tern is larger and has yellow tip to black bill.

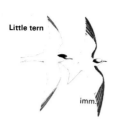

Little tern

imm.

LITTLE TERN
Sterna albifrons L24cm
Characteristics: The smallest of the sea-terns and easily identified by its white forehead and black-tipped yellow bill. Its short legs are a yellow-orange colour and the primaries are dark-tipped. Its dainty flight is interrupted by spells of hovering before plunging to catch small fish and shrimps. Dives are sometimes repeated many times in succession. It often gives the appearance of being suspended on invisible strings like a puppet. A chattering 'kree-ick' call is given in flight near the breeding colony and when fishing.

Distribution and habitat: Breeds in small widely-separated colonies on sandy or shingly islands on low-lying coasts, and sometimes inland in Europe. Commoner in southern areas and very scarce in Scandinavia. Migrates to African coast for the winter.

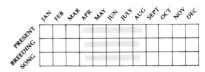

	JAN	FEB	MAR	APR	MAY	JUN	JULY	AUG	SEPT	OCT	NOV	DEC
PRESENT												
BREEDING												
SONG												

Habits and similar species: A lively bird when fishing, sometimes hovering in up-draughts and often calling excitedly when several birds are fishing together. Will take a variety of fish and shrimps in often quite shallow water and will fish in both freshwater and saltwater pools. So much smaller than other terns that may only be confused with winter plumage marsh terns which do not have yellow legs or bill.

53

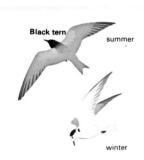

Black tern

summer

winter

BLACK TERN
Chlidonias niger L24cm
Characteristics: A small marsh tern, mostly dark in the summer with pale underwings and under-tail coverts, black legs and a black bill. Underside is white in winter and wings are greyer, but top of head retains small black patch. Colonies are filled with nasal 'kyeh kyeh' call and there is a shorter 'kit' call made by single birds.

Distribution and habitat: Breeds on freshwater lakes and wet marshes in sometimes large colonies. A very rare breeder in Bri- tain. Nests are usually made of floating vegetation fixed to marginal plants.

	JAN	FEB	MAR	APR	MAY	JUN	JULY	AUG	SEPT	OCT	NOV	DEC
PRESENT												
BREEDING												
SONG												

Habits and similar species: Catches flying insects over water, sometimes swooping to pick them from the surface, or pursuing them in flight. May catch small surface-feeding fish, but not by diving like Common or Arctic terns. White-winged Black Tern has dark body, but mainly white primaries and red bill. Whiskered Tern has red bill, greyer body and wings with white cheeks contrasting with black cap.

INLAND WATERS AND MARSHES

Freshwater lakes and rivers offer a variety of opportunities for feeding and birds have exploited most of them. Fish, invertebrates and aquatic plants are all taken by birds and there is a wide range of adaptations to take these foods. Diving, dabbling, wading and swimming all help birds get at their food in a watery environment.

Upland lakes and rivers are lowest in nutrients and support less freshwater life; as a result they support less birdlife, especially in winter, but lowland waters, richer in nutrients and freshwater life, support far more birds. A lowland lake with reed-fringed margins is an excellent bird habitat as it provides safe feeding, roosting and breeding sites. Many well-known nature reserves are located on lowland freshwater lakes or rivers.

Newly-created bodies of freshwater, such as gravel pits and reservoirs, also support many birds and they have led to a significant increase in the numbers of species like the Great Crested Grebe in certain areas. They are becoming increasingly important as bird habitats, especially for overwintering wildfowl.

Upland rivers are too fast flowing for many birds to be able to feed in them, but there are some exceptions and the Dipper has been able to exploit the food supply available in fast flowing hill streams by walking under the water. Lowland rivers with flooded meadows alongside them in winter attract wildfowl, sometimes in impressive numbers. They are attracted by the prospect of good feeding as these meadows are often very fertile and support a rich growth of grasses and clovers – ideal foods for geese.

An increasingly serious problem facing many bodies of freshwater is eutrophication, or enrichment of the water by agricultrual run-off. Fertilisers intended for crops drain through the soil and into the river systems, causing an increased growth in green algae. This prevents other plants from growing and often chokes the waterways, leading to a loss of fish and invertebrates, on which the birds feed.

A flock of Bewick Swans and Pochards on their winter feeding grounds.

55

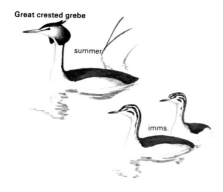

Great crested grebe

summer

imms.

GREAT CRESTED GREBE
Podiceps cristatus L50cm
Characteristics: Medium-sized long-necked diving bird with slender pointed bill. In summer both sexes have a conspicuous double-horned crest and white cheeks with rufous edges. The upperparts are dark throughout the year and the underside is always white; in winter the crest is almost completely absent and the cheeks are all white. A low crooning call is sometimes given, but there is also a more shrill barking call.

56

Distribution and habitat: A widespread breeding bird on lakes, ponds and slow rivers, usually where there is plenty of

marginal vegetation. In winter may be found in estuaries and on sheltered coasts. The nest is a floating platform of vegetation anchored to plants.

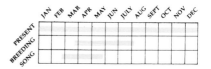

Habits and similar species: Catches fish by diving from the surface. The young, with boldly-striped heads, are often seen riding on the backs of one of the parents. Unable to walk on land. Elaborate courtship display involves much head shaking and calling, often with weed in the bill and the extraordinary 'penguin' dance when birds walk on the water. Red-necked Grebe is smaller with yellow at base of bill.

Red-necked grebe

summer

imm.

RED-NECKED GREBE
Podiceps grisegena L43cm
Characteristics: A medium-sized diving bird with a black and yellow bill. In summer the neck is a rich chestnut brown, the face is white and the head is black; there is no white line over the eye as in the Great Crested Grebe. In winter the face remains white and contrasts with the grey neck; the body and the neck have a stockier appearance than in the Great Crested Grebe. The squealing song is heard only on the breeding lakes, but there is a further high-pitched 'keck keck' often heard in winter.

Distribution and habitat: Breeds on lowland lakes with plenty of vegetation in central and eastern Europe. Migrates south and

west for the winter and many arrive at the coast, although some stay on large lakes and reservoirs.

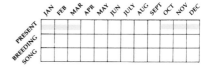

Habits and similar species: Dives from the surface for fish and small crustaceans, and takes aquatic insect larvae in the summer. Great Crested Grebe is larger with white neck in winter, Black-necked Grebe is smaller with upturned bill and Slavonian Grebe is smaller with pale tip to bill.

Little grebe

winter

imm.

summer

LITTLE GREBE
Tachybaptus ruficollis L27cm
Characteristics: The smallest European grebe with distinctive brown plumage, compact body and short neck. The chestnut cheeks and throat, and the bright gape patch at the base of the very short bill in summer prevent confusion with any other small grebe. In winter the cheeks and throat are a paler brown and the gape patch is less noticeable; fluffy tail feathers give a powder-puff appearance. Seldom flies but the wings show no trace of a wing bar or trailing white edge as in larger grebes. Song is a shrill whinnying trill, with a high 'whit whit' alarm note.

Distribution and habitat: A common and widespread bird, breeding on many types of freshwater habitat, especially on still and slow-moving water where there is plenty of marginal vegetation. The nest is a floating platform of weeds anchored to reed stems.

	JAN	FEB	MAR	APR	MAY	JUN	JULY	AUG	SEPT	OCT	NOV	DEC
PRESENT												
BREEDING												
SONG												

Habits and similar species: Dives from the surface for small fish, insect larvae and other invertebrates. Can be very difficult to see in breeding season; when disturbed slips off nest silently, covers eggs with weeds and then hides in vegetation. Black-necked Grebe is larger, paler in winter and has up-turned tip to bill. Slavonian Grebe is also larger and paler and has 'capped' effect with dark head and pale neck.

Black-necked grebe

imm.

summer

BLACK-NECKED GREBE
Podiceps nigricollis L30cm
Characteristics: A small grebe with a narrow all-black neck, a black back and golden-orange downwards-pointing ear-tufts. In winter the neck and underside are pale and the back is greyer. The short bill has an up-turned tip, making for easy identification in silhouette. In flight the wings show a trailing white edge. The call is a quiet 'pree-ip' and there is a more shrill-sounding chattering song.

Distribution and habitat: Very rare breeding bird in Scotland, commoner in Europe. Breeds on shallow ponds and small lakes, building a nest of floating plant stems. Sometimes nests in small colonies. In winter moves to larger lakes and reservoirs and also to the coast.

	JAN	FEB	MAR	APR	MAY	JUN	JULY	AUG	SEPT	OCT	NOV	DEC
PRESENT												
BREEDING												
SONG												

Habits and similar species: Dives from the surface for small fish, aquatic insect larvae and crustaceans. Easily separated from other grebes at all seasons by characteristic bill shape. Also crown is more pointed than flatter-headed Slavonian Grebe, and neck slightly longer than smaller Little Grebe.

58

MUTE SWAN
Cygnus olor L152cm

Characteristics: A very large and familiar all-white water-bird with an orange bill. The long neck is held in a curved position at rest but extended when in flight. The tail is pointed upwards slightly when swimming, and when feeding the body is up-ended in the water as it reaches the bottom with its long neck, feeding on aquatic plants. The wings produce a strong throbbing whistling sound in flight. Males have a large protuberance at the base of the bill; in females it is slightly smaller. Juveniles are greyish-brown with a darker bill and legs. A variety of hissing and grunting sounds are made by swimming birds, especially when intruders threaten the nest or the young. Usually solitary on the breeding site, but very large flocks exist in some areas.

Distribution and habitat: A widespread breeding bird on many types of freshwater habitat; prefers slow-moving or

still well-vegetated water. In winter may move to coast, sometimes congregating in flocks on sheltered estuaries.

Habits and similar species: Feeds on aquatic plants and marginal plants. Often raises its wings over body in display. Bewick's Swan smaller, black bill with yellow base. Whooper Swan same size, also black bill with yellow base.

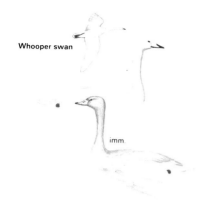

Whooper swan

imm

WHOOPER SWAN
Cygnus cygnus L155cm

Characteristics: The largest swan, with all white plumage, black legs and a yellow bill with black markings at the tip. The bill has a more triangular wedge shape, and there is no black protuberance at the base. Immatures are paler and greyer than immature Mute swans, and have a different shaped bill. The neck is held stiffly upright whilst swimming, and when up-ending the tail looks shorter and blunter.

Distribution and habitat: A shy bird at its breeding grounds in Iceland and far northern Europe. Nests on grassy tussocks in

swamps and on tundra lakes. Moves south for winter to coastal areas; often feeds on flooded meadows and coastal marshes, sometimes in large flocks.

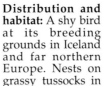

Habits and similar species: The call is a sad-sounding, far-carrying trumpeting sound, and a 'klo-klo-klo' flight call is also made. Sometimes birds on the water produce a song-like call of drawn-out notes. In flight the wings may make a gentle swishing, but they do not whistle like the Mute Swan. Bewick's Swan is much smaller with less yellow on the bill.

59

BEWICK'S SWAN
Cygnus columbianus L54cm

Characteristics: Like a small Whooper Swan with a shorter neck and less yellow on the bill; the yellow and black patches on the bill form patterns which are different in each swan and do not vary from year to year so individuals can easily be recognised. Calls are higher pitched and flight call sounds more like a double note 'kla-ow'.

Distribution and habitat: Breeds in far northern Scandinavia and Europe on tundra. In winter moves to large lakes and

flooded grasslands and feeds on grasses and other plants. Formerly the least common swan, but is showing signs of an increase.

Habits and similar species: A highly social bird in winter, with family groups keeping together after migration. Will sometimes feed in mixed flocks with Mute and Whooper Swans, and grey geese, often returning to the same sites year after year. Whooper Swan is much larger if the two are seen together. Longer neck and more yellow bill are best pointers for Whooper.

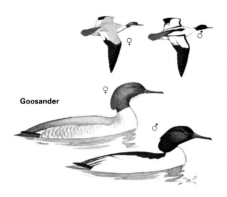

Goosander

GOOSANDER
Mergus merganser L64cm
Characteristics: A diving duck with a long, slender bill with a serrated edge and a slightly hooked tip. Males have a glossy green head, dark back and pinkish-buff underparts; in the summer this fades to white. Females are greyer with a reddish brown head showing a hint of a crest and a white throat. In flight males show a broad white wing panel; females have a trailing white patch with a darker surround.

60

Distribution and habitat: A widespread breeding bird in northern Britain and Europe; persecuted in some areas due to its

fish-eating habits. Nests in tree holes beside large clear rivers and lakes. In winter may move to the coast, but is more often seen on large lakes.

Habits and similar species: Dives for fish from the surface, using its serrated bill to grip them. May fish in organised groups driving prey into tight shoals. Male Red-breasted Merganser has crest on glossy green head and darker body and female is paler. No other diving birds, apart from much smaller Smew, have serrated, hooked-tip bill.

Moorhen

imm.

MOORHEN
Gallinula chloropus L33cm
Characteristics: A compact dark-bodied water-bird with a white line along the side and white under-tail coverts. The yellow-tipped bill has a red base and the legs are bright yellow-green. When walking and swimming the tail is constantly flicked, revealing the white underside and the head bobs in a clockwork-toy fashion. In flight the legs dangle below the body, but the normal method of escape is to run, so this is not always seen. A loud and far-carrying 'kirrick' is the usual call.

Distribution and habitat: A widespread and common breeding bird found beside many types of freshwater habitat ranging

from tiny ponds and ditches to large lakes and rivers, although almost always where there is plenty of marginal vegetation.

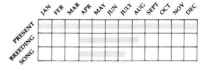

Habits and similar species: Usually fairly secretive, feeding at the edges of ponds and rivers where it can easily dash for cover. Usually nests close to water in thick vegetation. May sometimes emerge into open fields at dawn or dusk. Eats a wide range of plant and animal material and may become relatively tame in urban parks taking scraps from people. The Coot is all black with a white bill and forehead.

Coot

imm.

Distribution and habitat: A common and widespread breeding bird on lakes and rivers which have a good depth of vegetation on the margins. In winter large flocks may gather on larger more open stretches of water; in' hard weather some migrate to the coast.

	JAN	FEB	MAR	APR	MAY	JUN	JULY	AUG	SEPT	OCT	NOV	DEC
PRESENT												
BREEDING												
SONG												

COOT
Fulica atra L38cm

Characteristics: An all-black medium-sized waterbird with a short white bill and a white frontal plate on the head. The wing has a trailing white edge which is just visible in flight. The feet have lobed toes and the greenish legs trail behind the body in flight. A loud, piercing 'kewk' or 'cut' call is given from time to time.

Habits and similar species: A gregarious bird, but also quite quarrelsome, often engaging in noisy and splashy chases. Picks food from the surface, but dives freely as well, feeding on a variety of plant and animal material. Nests close to water, usually hidden in reeds. Moorhen has red and yellow bill and white stripe along side of body.

61

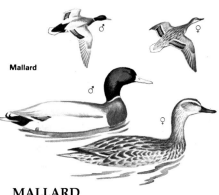
Mallard

♂

♀

♂

♀

Distribution and habitat: A very common breeding bird on a wide range of freshwater habitats, sometimes on urban park lakes. In winter there is some movement away from upland areas and many birds overwinter at the coast.

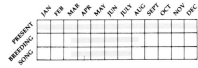

	JAN	FEB	MAR	APR	MAY	JUN	JULY	AUG	SEPT	OCT	NOV	DEC
PRESENT												
BREEDING												
SONG												

MALLARD
Anas platyrhynchos L58cm

Characteristics: The largest freshwater duck. Drakes have a glossy green head with a narrow white collar and a yellow bill. The chestnut breast and grey and black upperparts are varied in domesticated and hybrid birds, but wild birds are more uniformly marked. The duck is a more uniform speckled brown with a white-edged dark blue speculum or wing patch. The usual call is the familiar 'quack', uttered by the ducks; drakes have a quieter 'queep'.

Habits and similar species: Drakes court the ducks in winter with a variety of quiet whistling calls and a head-bobbing display. Mallards feed by dabbling in shallow water and by up-ending, taking a variety of plant materials and small invertebrates. Nests are usually well concealed, sometimes in dense vegetation. Drake Shoveler has a glossy green head, but the breast is white and the flanks are chestnut.

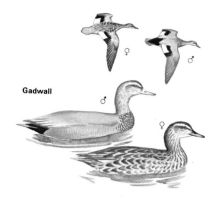

Gadwall

GADWALL
Anas strepera L51cm
Characteristics: The drake is the least conspicuous dabbling duck with mainly grey upperparts, with a chestnut wing patch and black tail coverts. Bill is shorter than Mallard's and greyish. Duck is a slim version of a duck Mallard with a black and white speculum. In flight both sexes show a white belly and black and white wing patches. The usual call of the drake is a deep nasal quack; the duck has a quieter version of the Mallard's quack.

Distribution and habitat: A widespread but never very common breeding bird, nesting on lowland marshes, usually freshwater but sometimes brackish. Northern and eastern breeding birds migrate south and west for the winter favouring weedy lakes and marshes.

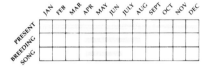

Habits and similar species: A fairly shy bird, often flying off for a great distance when disturbed. Feeds on aquatic plants by dabbling and up-ending. The nest is built close to the water in thick vegetation. May gather in large flocks in winter on suitable lakes. Drake Wigeon is smaller and greyish with black tail coverts, but has chestnut head and peach-coloured crown.

Wigeon

WIGEON
Anas penelope L46cm
Characteristics: A medium-sized dabbling duck with a short bill. Drake has grey upperparts with black tail coverts and white stripe along the wings. The chestnut head and peach-coloured crown are distinctive; in flight the white forewing is very conspicuous. Duck is a smaller, neater version of the duck Mallard with a small green speculum and short pointed tail. Drake's whistling 'whee-oo' call is far-carrying.

Distribution and habitat: A fairly common breeding bird on freshwater pools and lakes on moorland and tundra in northern Britain, Iceland and northern Europe. In winter is more likely to be found in large flocks further south on estuaries and coastal marshes.

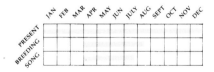

Habits and similar species: Feeds on grasses, roots and leaves by grazing, but also on aquatic plants by dabbling in shallow water. Nests on the ground, or on tiny islands in lakes. American Wigeon is a rare trans-Atlantic visitor; drake has green, white and buff head and browner upperparts. Duck is very similar to duck Wigeon, but at close range shows a greyer head and neck, and in flight has white axillaries.

Teal

TEAL
Anas crecca L35cm
Characteristics: The smallest duck with a fast wader-like flight. The drake's chestnut head has a broad green stripe running through the eye. A horizontal white stripe along the wing is conspicuous on sitting birds. The duck resembles a small compact duck mallard with a small green speculum. Broad white patches below the wings show well in flight. The drake has a high-pitched whistling call and the duck makes a rather harsh sounding 'quack'.

Distribution and habitat: A widespread and sometimes common breeder, although often absent from quite large areas. Usually nests beside well-vegetated lakes or large slow rivers, moving to flood-meadows and more coastal areas in winter.

Habits and similar species: A gregarious species, often feeding in quite large flocks in winter. In flight flocks may engage in aerobatics like a flock of waders. Green-winged Teal, a rare vagrant from North America, has a vertical white stripe on side of body and lacks the horizontal white stripe above the wings. Garganey is also very small, but has white stripe over eye.

63

Garganey

GARGANEY
Anas querquedula L38cm
Characteristics: Only slightly larger than the Teal, with a longer and broader bill. The drake has a conspicuous white stripe above the eye and a blue-grey forewing, with the rest of the upperparts being mainly dark speckled brown. The duck has a more speckled appearance than the duck Teal, a whiter throat, and a faint eye-stripe. The drake produces a curious rattling call, but the duck makes a more familiar quiet 'quack'.

Distribution and habitat: An uncommon summer visitor to reedy lowland lakes and freshwater marshes, nesting on the ground in dense vegetation. Confined mainly to southern Britain and central Europe. May occur on coastal marshes on migration in spring and autumn.

Habits and similar species: Not as sociable as the Teal, rarely being found in large flocks. Feeds on a variety of plants and invertebrates by dabbling and grazing at the edge of marshes. Blue-winged Teal is a rare vagrant from North America. Drake has a dark blue head with a white crescent in front of the eye. Duck is much more difficult to identify, but has blue speculum and bluish forewing.

Pintail

PINTAIL
Anas acuta L66cm

Characteristics: A large dabbling duck, commoner in the north. The drake has a striking head pattern of brown and white with a blue bill. The underside is white, merging into the greyer back. The neck looks longer than in other dabbling ducks and the central tail feathers are greatly elongated. The duck is paler brown than the duck mallard with a barely visible bronze-coloured speculum.

Distribution and habitat: A rare breeding bird in northern Britain, becoming much commoner in Iceland and Scandinavia. Nests beside lakes or on marshes, moving south for the winter. Usually present on coastal marshes in winter; sometimes inland on flood-meadows.

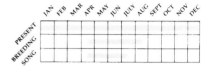

Habits and similar species: Feeds on a wide range of plant and animal material, including roots, seeds, insects, earthworms and tiny crustaceans. Duck resembles duck Wigeon, but is paler with more slender neck and indistinct speculum. Long-tailed Duck is much smaller with longer tail and white head and neck.

Shoveler

SHOVELER
Anas clypeata L51cm

Characteristics: Easily recognised by its broad, spade-ended bill, present in both sexes. In flight and at rest the heavy bill gives a down-tilted appearance to the head. Drake has a glossy green head, white breast, chestnut-orange flanks and a blue forewing. Duck is a pale speckled brown with a green speculum and blue forewing. Drake gives a nasal, di-syllabic 'chook-OOK' call, and the duck produces a more Mallard-like di-syllabic quack.

Distribution and habitat: A widespread, sometimes common breeding bird, being a summer visitor only to northern Britain, Iceland and central Europe. Breeds on water-meadows and marshes. In winter may gather in quite large flocks inland on flood-meadows and lakes.

Habits and similar species: Can be secretive, keeping to well-vegetated margins. Broad bill is used to sieve through water and liquid mud for tiny invertebrates and seeds. Drake's wings make slight rattling sound when taking off. Drake Mallard has green head, but does not have white front and bill is conventionally shaped. Duck can not be confused with other ducks when bill is clearly seen.

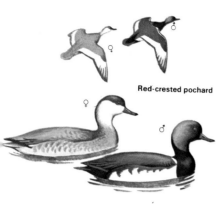

Red-crested pochard

Tufted duck

RED-CRESTED POCHARD
Netta rufina L56cm
Characteristics: A medium-sized diving duck. The drake has a red bill and red legs, and a chestnut-orange head with slightly raised feathers on the crown. The duck has a pale, off-white cheek and a dark crown and only the tip of the bill is a pinkish-red colour. In flight the drake looks dark with contrasting brown wings with a large pale wingbar. The underwing is white with large white axillaries.

Distribution and habitat: A very scarce breeding bird in Britain, usually occurring as a vagrant. Many sightings will be of escapes from wildfowl collections. Breeds by well-vegetated lakes in Europe, moving south and west for the winter.

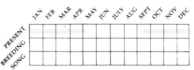

Habits and similar species: Feeds by up-ending and diving, taking mainly aquatic vegetation. Runs along the surface of the water to take off. Pochard drake has chestnut head and black chest, but grey back and flanks and dark bill. Female Long-tailed Duck similar, but compare facial markings, bill shape and darker breast.

TUFTED DUCK
Aythya fuligula L43cm
Characteristics: A medium-sized diving duck. The drake is mostly glossy black with white sides. The purple tinged head has a drooping crest and the grey bill has a black tip. The duck is a more uniform brown, but may show white under-tail coverts. There may also be a white band at the base of the bill, and the crest is much smaller. Both sexes have a bright yellow eye.

Distribution and habitat: A widespread and, in some areas, common breeding bird, nesting by freshwater ponds and lakes. Nest is usually well concealed on the ground near the water, hidden by dense vegetation. In winter is more likely to be seen on larger lakes.

Habits and similar species: Dives from the surface for bottom-dwelling molluscs, invertebrates and plants. Drake Scaup has glossy green head, no crest and dark grey back. Duck Scaup has broader white band at base of bill. Drake Ring-necked Duck, a rare vagrant from N. America, has no crest, two white bands across bill and vertical white stripe on flanks. Duck has peaked head, pale patch at base of bill.

65

Pochard

POCHARD
Aythya ferina L46cm

Characteristics: A medium-sized diving duck. Drake has a chestnut head, black chest and tail, and grey upperparts. The duck is brown, with paler colourings on the back and wings. In flight both sexes show an indistinct pale wing bar, and both have a blue-grey bill with a black tip. In profile the head shape appears triangular with a broad, slightly flattened bill. The varied calls include a number of deep wheezing and whistling sounds.

Distribution and habitat: A fairly common breeding bird over a wide area, preferring large lakes and reservoirs with reedy margins. The nest is usually concealed in a reed bed. In winter moves to more open waters, including large semi-urban reservoirs.

Habits and similar species: Dives for small invertebrates, sometimes in quite deep water; also feeds on aquatic plants. Spends most of its time on the water, often sleeping far out on deep lakes. Red-crested Pochard has red bill and brighter chestnut head. Drake Ferruginous Duck is all chestnut-brown with white eye; duck is brown with white under-tail coverts. Both sexes show prominent white wing bars.

66

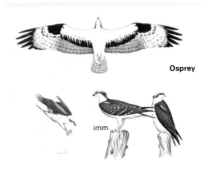

Osprey

imm.

OSPREY
Pandion haliaetus L55cm

Characteristics: A large bird of prey with brown upperparts, a white underside and a bold brown facial stripe. In flight the wings look long and angled; the usual flight pattern is to fly slowly over water with deep flapping wing-beats, but soaring and hovering also occur. Perching on dead trees or posts in water is also commonly seen. When prey is sighted the wings are swept back and a steep dive into the water follows; the feet enter the water first to capture the prey. The sexes are alike, but juveniles are more mottled.

Distribution and habitat: A scarce summer visitor to Scotland, but commoner in northern Europe and Scandinavia. Usually nests in large conifer tree in wooded or upland regions near large lakes and rivers. During migration may occur in many freshwater habitats.

Habits and similar species: Skilled at catching large fish, having specially adapted feet and claws to grip with, and is able to take off from the water with heavy prey. Makes a shrill cheeping and yelping call. Marsh Harrier also flies low over water, but is pale headed and has dark underside. White-tailed Eagle is much larger (up to 90cm) and is all dark underneath.

Kingfisher

KINGFISHER
Alcedo atthis L16cm

Characteristics: A small but brilliantly coloured water bird with a compact body, a short tail and a long bill. The Kingfisher is unmistakable with its iridescent blue-green back and bright chestnut-orange underside. The bill which seems very large in proportion to the body is black, but in females the base of the lower mandible is red. There is a small white patch on the sides of the neck and below the bill. The short legs are red. Shrill and far-carrying whistling calls are given as Kingfishers dash over the water and sometimes overland or even through trees. Song is a quiet trilling whistle.

Distribution and habitat: A widespread breeding bird in southern Britain, Europe and southern Sweden, occurring on a wide variety of unpolluted waters where small fish can be found. In winter may be found on the coast and beside estuaries.

Habits and similar species: Dives for small fish from a perch or sometimes after hovering. Often uses a favourite perch regularly. Nests in deep holes in steep banks; when occupied these holes become smelly and soiled with droppings. No other European bird has the same colourings, but Roller, which is much larger (31cm) has brown back and blue underside.

67

Sand martin

SAND MARTIN
Riparia riparia L12cm

Characteristics: The smallest swallow with sandy-brown upperparts and a brown breast-band on a white underside. The short tail has a slight fork and the wings have greyish primaries and secondaries on the underside. A nasal twittering song is a repetitive version of the short call. Usually seen flying low over water in small feeding flocks.

Distribution and habitat: Absent from many of its former locations due to habitat loss or damage to breeding sites, but still found over a very wide area, as far as northern Scandinavia, especially where there is open water to feed over and steep sandy banks to nest in.

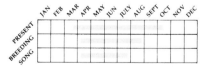

Habits and similar species: Digs a burrow up to 1m deep in sandy banks, usually near water. Catches insects on the wing. In autumn migrates to southern Africa. Crag Martin has buff underside and spots below the tail. House martin is black above with white rump and white underside.

Heron

GREY HERON
Ardea cinerea L90cm

Characteristics: A large grey and white water bird with long legs and a dagger-like bill. Usually seen standing motionless with neck either stretched out or hunched up. Head and neck are white with black streaks; has a long black crest. In flight it makes slow deep wingbeats, resembling large bird of prey. Neck is retracted in flight giving a front-heavy appearance. When startled, and at breeding colony, herons make a deep, grating 'kraaank'.

68

Distribution and habitat: Found over a very wide area, but less common in far north, breeding wherever there is water to fish and suitable nest sites. In winter may move away from some inland and upland areas to coastal regions, especially estuaries and sheltered bays.

Habits and similar species: Fishes by stalking or waiting patiently until the prey can be caught by a rapid movement of the bill. Usually feeds on fish, but will also take waterbirds and small mammals. Purple Heron has reddish neck and darker upperparts and is smaller and more slender. Much more secretive than Grey Heron remaining in dense reeds for longer periods.

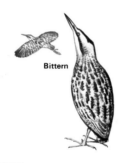

Bittern

BITTERN
Botaurus stellaris L75cm

Characteristics: A very secretive bird, far more often heard than seen. Like a plump brown heron with a black cap and shorter greenish legs. The mottled brown plumage blends perfectly with the reed beds which it spends most of its time in. Usually walks slowly through the reeds, sometimes above the water level by clutching bunches of reeds in its feet. Sometimes glimpsed in flight, looking like a large brown owl, early in the morning as it flies to its feeding grounds. The deep booming call usually heard at night.

Distribution and habitat: An uncommon breeding bird in southern Britain and Europe, restricted to dense reed beds and well-vegetated fens and swamps. In winter, Bitterns may move southwards to more open waters in order to avoid ice.

Habits and similar species: Stalks slowly and silently through reed beds in search of fish, but will also take small mammals, amphibians, reptiles and nestling birds. American Bittern is a very scarce vagrant, lacking black crown, but with black stripes down sides of whiter neck. Little Bittern is much smaller (35cm) with conspicuous black and buff wings. Female is like a small bittern with buff wing patches.

Marsh harrier
upper views

♀

♂

MARSH HARRIER
Circus aeruginosus L48-56cm
Characteristics: The largest European harrier with broader wings and a less buoyant flight than other harriers. The size difference between the sexes is less marked than in other harriers and the colourings are more alike. The smaller male has a grey tail and mostly grey wings with a pale head. The larger female is browner with a very pale head and a pale leading edge to the wing. In display a harsh almost lapwing-like 'kee-eek' call is made and the alarm call is a harsh and repetetive 'kek kek'.

Distribution and habitat: A very rare breeding bird in southern England, becoming more common in south and west Europe. Prefers reedy marshes and extensive reed beds bordering large lakes, but may also be seen hunting over rough grassland and cultivated fields.

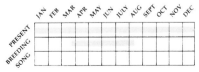

Habits and similar species: Hunts for small mammals and birds by flying low over reed beds or drier land; may also scavenge. Occasionally soars, looking rather like Buzzard. Buzzard has broader wings and shorter, more rounded tail. Black Kite has shorter, more rounded wings and slightly forked tail. Male Hen Harrier slimmer with grey back and dark wing-tips; female brown, dark head and pale rump.

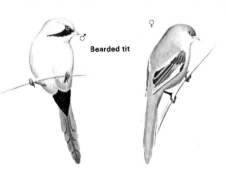

♂
Bearded tit
♀

BEARDED TIT
Panurus biarmicus L16.5cm
Characteristics: The only very small bird with a very long tail likely to be seen in a reed bed. Both sexes mostly reddish-brown, but males have a grey head with dark moustachial stripes and dark under-tail coverts. Females have pale buff colourings on head and lack the moustachial stripes. Both have a yellow bill and black legs. The most familiar call is a metallic 'ping', but quieter twittering calls are also made. Flight in open is weak and undulating.

Distribution and habitat: A scarce breeding bird in southern England and scattered localities in Europe, being confined to *Phragmites* beds. The Bearded Tit is greatly at risk from habitat destruction, and in addition suffers badly in severe winters.

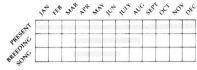

Habits and similar species: Feeds on tiny seeds and small insects, especially in summer when feeding young and the new season's seeds have not developed. Nests low down in a reed bed, making a tiny cup of woven leaves. In autumn may gather in larger flocks and may be seen in flight high above reed beds. Penduline Tit has shorter tail and white head and black eye patches meeting over bill.

Water rail

imm.

WATER RAIL
Rallus aquaticus L28cm
Characteristics: A common, but difficult to observe inhabitant of reed beds and marshes, usually betrayed by its strange, pig-like squeals and grunts, heard mainly at dawn and dusk. Sexes are alike, having brown upperparts, a grey underside and beautifully striped flanks. The long, slightly downcurved bill is bright red with a darker tip. The tail is usually held up and flicked revealing the white underside. In flight the legs trail and the head is extended.

Distribution and habitat: A widespread breeding bird of many freshwater habitats, but difficult to census. May turn

up in unusual habitats, like offshore islands, on migration. May feed a short distance out in the open in winter, but scuttles for cover if disturbed.

Habits and similar species: Feeds on many types of freshwater invertebrate, and will also take small fish and some plant material. May even scavenge in very harsh weather. Can easily move between reed stems without betraying its presence and climbs well over obstacles. Spotted Crake is smaller and has shorter yellow bill. Moorhen is all black with white stripe on flanks and short red and yellow bill.

SPOTTED CRAKE
Porzana porzana L23cm
Characteristics: A rare and even more secretive reed-bed inhabitant than the Water Rail. The bill is short and yellowish-green and the grey underside is spotted with white. The barring on the flanks is less distinct and the legs are greenish. The so-called whiplash call, a quiet 'hwitt hwitt' may be the only hint of its presence, and a snipe-like, di-syllabic call is also heard.

Distribution and habitat: A very rare breeding bird in Scotland, commoner in Europe and the extreme south of Scandina-

via. Dense reed beds and well-vegetated marshes are used for nesting and feeding, making observations very difficult.

Habits and similar species: A highly secretive bird, difficult to observe, but sometimes glimpsed feeding at base of reeds on small invertebrates and plant scraps. Little Crake is smaller (19cm) with similar proportions but grey, unspotted flanks. Baillon's Crake is smaller still (18cm) and has barred flanks, white streaks on wing coverts and greyish-pink legs.

71

Reed warbler

Distribution and habitat:

A common summer visitor to reed beds and well-vegetated river and lake shores, and occasionally drier habitats such as hedgerows. Reed Warblers breed in southern Britain, Europe and Scandinavia.

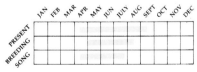

REED WARBLER
Acrocephalus scirpaceus L12.5cm

Characteristics: Easier to locate and identify by its song than by its appearance, it spends most of its time in dense reed beds. Its brown upperparts and pale underside help it blend with reed stems. The throat is usually the palest part of the underside. Its song is a repetitive combination of harsh notes, usually sounding like 'jurr jurr jurr chirruc chirruc chirruc'. When birds are present in high density, the songs merge into an insect-like buzz.

Habits and similar species: Occasionally seen feeding at edge of the reeds, and sometimes sings from a prominent perch, but usually remains in the reeds. Feeds on a variety of insects and spiders, climbing up and down reed stems with agility. Nest woven from grasses and suspended from a reed. Marsh Warbler is almost identical, but has a much more varied song with mimicry of other birds songs and calls.

Savi's warbler

Distribution and habitat: A very rare summer visitor to southern Britain, but commoner in Europe. Confined to reed beds and marshes, usually nesting near to the water level on a dense mat of vegetation.

SAVI'S WARBLER
Locustella luscinioides L14cm
Characteristics: Usually detected by its unusual song; a long, drawn-out reeling sound, often preceded by sharp ticking notes. Song is given in bursts with occasional scolding notes in between. The upperparts are a rufous brown without any distinguishing marks and the underside is paler with a white chin.

Habits and similar species: May be seen perched in the reeds with its rounded tail bobbing; is usually less secretive than other reed-bed warblers. Feeds on insects picked from reed stems. Grasshopper Warbler has similar song, but has less rufous streaked upperparts, and is more secretive. Great Reed Warbler is much larger with loud rasping song.

Great reed warbler

GREAT REED WARBLER
Acrocephalus arundinaceus L19cm
Characteristics: A very large warber with a loud rasping song, often delivered from a prominent perch in the reed bed. The song is repetetive with many harsh, deep frog-like croaks, sounding like 'kura kura kura, krik krik krik, gurk gurk gurk'. There is less mimicry in the song than in the other warblers. The bill looks stout compared with Reed Warbler, but the body colourings are almost identical; the eye-stripe is slightly more prominent.

Distribution and habitat: A very rare visitor to Britain on migration, and not a breeding bird. In southern Europe may nest colonially in reed beds and other freshwater margins. The large nest of woven grasses is suspended from reed stems and leaves.

Habits and similar species: Apart from its size, a typical insect-eating warbler. Migrates south in autumn to Africa. Reed Warbler is smaller with quieter and less grating song. Cetti's Warbler is smaller and darker above, with explosive, chirruping song.

MARSH WARBLER
Acrocephalus palustris L12.5cm
Characteristics: Almost identical to Reed Warbler and best distinguished by song. Usual song contains a great deal of skilled mimicry, and is louder and more musical than either Reed or Sedge Warbler. It may be delivered from a more prominent perch and may continue into the night. Upperparts can appear more olive-brown than the Reed Warbler and throat is more obviously white. The legs are pinkish, unlike Reed Warbler's which are dark.

Distribution and habitat: A very scarce and declining summer visitor to Britain, but commoner in Europe and southern Scandinavia. Usually nests in thick vegetation near water, sometimes in cornfields or hedgerows. Nest of grasses and animal hair hung from vegetation.

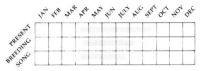

Habits and similar species: Like other reed warblers is difficult to observe, spending much of its time in dense vegetation, but may be seen when singing. Grasshopper Warbler also occurs in dense grassy areas away from water; it has streaked upperparts and a more rounded tail and produces a prolonged reeling call.

Sedge warbler

Distribution and habitat: A widespread and common summer visitor, occurring all over Britain and Europe in a variety of damp and well-vegetated habitats, often near water, but sometimes also found in hedgrows and along damp ditches.

SEDGE WARBLER
Acrocephalus schoenobaenas L13cm
Characteristics: More striking in appearance than some of the other reed bed warblers with a prominent eye-stripe, dark legs, slightly streaked upperparts and an un-streaked orange rump. The song is a mixture of trills, melodious and harsh-sounding notes and contains some mimicry. There are also some scolding notes and a sharp 'tucc'.

Habits and similar species: The nest is built near to ground level and is a deep cup of grasses, sometimes lined with cobwebs and feathers. A variety of insects are taken as food. The Aquatic Warbler has a similar eye-stripe and a buff crown stripe; the orange rump is streaked and the legs are a pale pink. The song is composed of shorter more distinct phrases.

Cetti's warbler

CETTI'S WARBLER
Cettia cetti L14cm

Characteristics: A very secretive inhabitant of reed beds, far more often heard than seen. If seen, upperparts look dark brown and unstreaked and contrast strongly with greyish-white underside. A pale stripe above the eye separates the darker crown from the paler face, giving the impression of a wren. The broad tail is rounded at the tip and looks slightly ruffled. The explosive song is given from a well concealed perch, usually a bush within a reed bed and is reminiscent of a wren, but it begins and ends abruptly. Also has a number of harsh alarm notes.

Distribution and habitat: A recent coloniser of reed-beds, densely-vegetated ditches and riversides in southern Britain, commoner in similar habitats in both south and west Europe. Cetti's Warbler may be expanding its range northwards.

Habits and similar species: Feeds on insects caught deep in reed beds, often near the water. Flicks its tail downwards or sideways whilst perched. Non-migratory over most of its range.

Reed bunting

♀

♂

REED BUNTING
Emberiza schoeniclus L15.5cms

Characteristics: In the breeding season the male has a striking black hood with white moustachial stripes which merge to form a band around the nape. In winter the black hood moults to become browner but is still distinctive. Females have a browner head and streaked brown upperparts. The outer tail feathers are white in both sexes. Various short calls are made and males sing their squeaky and rather jerky song from a prominent perch.

Distribution and habitat: A widespread, sometimes common, resident bird over Britain and Europe, being mostly migratory in Scandinavia. Breeds in reed beds, damp field edges, riversides and drier habitats like hedgerows. May move to farmland or suburban areas in winter.

Habits and similar species: Feeds on small seeds and insects collected from the vegetation and on the ground. May gather in small flocks, joining forces with other buntings and finches in winter. Male Rustic Bunting (L14.5cm) has black hood but white throat and chestnut breast band; in winter cheeks are chestnut.

Greylag goose

Distribution and habitat: A widespread but not common breeding bird in northern and eastern Britain, probably commonest in Scotland. The Greylag Goose breeds colonially on marshes and islands in lakes, moving onto farmland in winter.

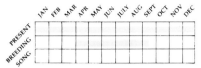

GREYLAG GOOSE
Anser anser L76-89cm

Characteristics: One of the largest 'grey' geese with an orange bill, pink legs and light grey forewings which show well in flight. The head and neck look pale compared with other grey geese. Appears heavy and ponderous on the ground and in flight. The clamorous 'kyang-ung-ung' flight call helps distinguish Greylags flying in mixed flocks or in poor light. A typical cackling goose call and a loud hissing is given by birds on the ground.

Habits and similar species: A highly gregarious species, sometimes forming mixed flocks with other grey geese. Feeds on a variety of plant material, especially the roots of grasses and other meadow plants. Pink-footed Goose also has pink feet, but has darker head and neck and pink bill. Bean Goose has orange legs and orange-yellow bill.

75

Pink-footed goose

Distribution and habitat: Breeds in small colonies on open tundra and rocky ground in Svalbard, Iceland and Greenland. The latter two populations overwinter in Britain and western Europe, mainly on farmland and freshwater marshes, but sometimes on coastal marshes.

PINK-FOOTED GOOSE
Anser brachyrhynchus L60-75cm

Characteristics: A large grey goose with pink legs and a dark bill with pink patches near the tip. The head is noticeably darker than the rest of the body and the upperparts have an almost 'frosted' blue-grey tinge. In flight the underwings look much darker than the underside of the body. A very vocal goose with a variety of calls; the most frequently heard is a short, trumpeting 'ank ank' call.

Habits and similar species: Feeds by day on grasses, seeds and sometimes crops, and roosts at night on large lakes or estuaries, often engaging in a spectacular mass fly-past. Bean Goose has orange legs and bill and darker forewings in flight. Greylag Goose has paler head and pale forewings in flight. White-fronted Goose has pink bill with no black areas, and white patch surrounding bill.

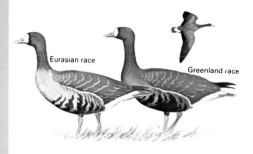

Eurasian race

Greenland race

WHITE-FRONTED GOOSE
Anser albifrons L70cm
Characteristics: A large grey goose with a pink bill and orange legs. Adults have a distinctive white forehead and dark barring on the underside, making them easier to identify than other grey geese. Juveniles lack barring and white forehead but still have pink bill and orange legs. Birds which breed in Greenland and overwinter in north-west Britain have a slightly larger and stronger bill which is yellowish-orange. In flight wings do not show pale patches as in the Greylag or Pink-foot. Cackling call notes higher-pitched than other grey geese.

Distribution and habitat: Breeds in colonies on Arctic tundra in Greenland and far northern Europe. In winter Greenland

race migrates to north-west Britain; Eurasian birds migrate to southern Britain and western Europe and are usually less numerous.

Habits and similar species: The very rare Lesser White-fronted Goose is smaller (53-66cm) with a shorter bill and a more peaked forehead. The area of white on the forehead is larger, extending further back onto the head and there is a distinctive yellow eye-ring, visible at long range. The plumage is generally darker. A single bird may sometimes turn up with a much larger flock of White-fronts.

Barnacle goose

BARNACLE GOOSE
Branta leucopsis L63cm
Characteristics: A medium-sized black goose with black legs and an all-white face. The black crown and neck contrast strongly with the white underside, making a useful field identification characteristic in flight. The grey upperparts are strongly barred with black, white and grey in both adults and juveniles. The gruff, yelping 'gak' or 'ark' calls are rather like the barking of a small dog, but when large flocks are calling the effect is of a deep roaring sound.

Distribution and habitat: A winter visitor to north-west Britain, Ireland and the Netherlands, feeding on saltmarshes

and coastal grasslands. Breeds on rocky ledges and offshore islets on Greenland, Svalbard and Novaya Zemlaya, often in large colonies.

Habits and similar species: Single birds are usually escapes from ornamental wildfowl collections; large feeding flocks remain isolated from other geese. Brent Goose is smaller and has all dark face. Canada Goose is larger and browner above, and has broad white 'chin-strap'. Red-breasted Goose has small white facial patch, but chestnut breast and black underside with white stripe below wings.

CRANE
Grus grus L115cm

Characteristics: A very large heron-like bird with a black-and-white head and neck and a small red cap. The bill is shorter than heron's, but legs are as long. Short tail is mostly hidden by a tuft of short plumes. In flight, neck is fully extended and underwing shows a broad black trailing edge, formed by black tips to the primaries and secondaries. Grey Heron lacks the black underwing, flies with neck retracted.

Distribution and habitat: A very rare breeding bird in Britain, becoming commoner in northern Europe and Scandinavia. Nest is mound of vegetation on the ground in swampy areas, sometimes in woodland. In winter they move to margins of lakes and wettish farmland.

Habits and similar species: Feeds on a variety of plant foods collected from the ground; also invertebrates, amphibians, small birds and mammals. Sometimes in large flocks or flying in loose V-formation or long lines. Demoiselle Crane much smaller (L96cm), white ear tufts, black head and breast plumes and no red on head. Saurus Crane is larger (L156cm), has bare red skin on head and neck and grey crown.

Jack snipe

JACK SNIPE
Lymnocryptes minimus L19cm

Characteristics: A small brown wader with a short straight bill and short legs. The crown is brown, but the back shows two conspicuous yellowish stripes. Usually difficult to observe on the ground, breaking cover only when aproached very closely. Unlike Snipe, it is normally silent when flushed and flies more directly, often dropping quickly out of sight. The tail is pointed and lacks any white in it. Usually there is no call when flushed, but sometimes a quiet single note is heard. The display call has been likened to a muffled galloping sound of distant horses.

Distribution and habitat: A widespread breeding bird in far northern Europe and Scandinavia, nesting in wet swamps and boggy areas. Migrates south and west in winter, often visiting drier tussocky grassland than Snipe. Not usually found in large numbers.

Habits and similar species: A secretive bird, even away from the breeding sites, but can sometimes be glimpsed at edge of boggy pools. Has curious habit of bobbing up and down like a Dipper. Snipe is larger with much longer straight bill. Great Snipe is larger (L28cm) with slightly longer bill and broad tail with conspicuous areas of white in it.

MARSHES & WETLANDS

77

Snipe

Distribution and habitat: A widespread, sometimes common, breeding bird over most of the region; usually present through-out year. Nests in low vegetation in various wetland habitats, sometimes at high altitudes. In winter moves to marshes, lake margins or flood meadows.

SNIPE
Gallinago gallinago L27cm
Characteristics: A small brown wader with short legs and an extremely long straight bill, longer in proportion than any other European bird. The brown head has a pale central crown stripe and the underside is white. In flight a pale trailing edge to the wing is just visible. When flushed rises rapidly, uttering a short sneeze-like call, then flies in a rapid zig-zag fashion with stong wing beats. Display flight is high and involves diving at a 45° angle; protruding tail feathers produce loud bleating call. Seen perched on posts or tussocks making squeaky 'chip-per' call.

Habits and similar species: Feeds on a range of invertebrates, especially earthworms which are detected by the sensitive tip to the bill. Usually feeds in small flocks, often flying together in close formation. Jack Snipe is smaller with much shorter bill and more direct flight. Woodcock is larger (L34cm) and plumper with shorter bill and legs, barred underside and barred crown.

78

Little ringed plover

Distribution and habitat: A scarce breeding bird in southern Britain, becoming commoner in Europe. Breeds beside freshwater pools and rivers where there are expanses of rough sand and gravel to nest on. In winter may move to the coast.

LITTLE RINGED PLOVER
Charadrius dubius L15cm
Characteristics: A small short-billed wader with a striking black and white head pattern. Above the black forehead is a thin, white line and there is a yellow eye ring. Together with the lack of any wing bars these make useful characteristics for separating this species from the slightly larger Ringed Plover. Also, the bill is all black and the legs are dull yellow rather than orange. A di-syllabic, descending 'pee-u' call is sometimes given from the ground and the display song is a more trilling version of this and other short calls. The sandy colourings of the upperparts make this a very difficult bird to see when it is sitting quietly.

Habits and similar species: Feeds on a variety of invertebrates caught by running after them on gravel and shingle by freshwater, and sometimes on very dry habitats. Usually solitary or in very small groups. Ringed Plover is larger (L19cm) and lacks eye-ring and white line above black forehead. Kentish Plover has black legs and lacks black breast band; it has a much smaller area of black on face.

Lapwing

imm

LAPWING
Vanellus vanellus L30cm
Characteristics: Common wader with striking black crest. Crown, face and chest are black, but nape and underside are white. Upperparts look black at a distance and in flight, but in good sunlight and at closer range are seen to be a deep glossy green, explaining the other English name, 'Green Plover'. The under-tail coverts are orange. They are sociable, conspicuous birds with a loud 'pee-wit' call (giving it its third English name). Display flight involves much acrobatic rolling, soaring and diving, showing off broad wings.

Distribution and habitat: A widespread, once common breeding bird in Britain and Europe; declining due to drainage and intensive agriculture. Breeds on grasslands, heathland and moorlands, sometimes on drier marshes near sea, nesting in shallow scrape.

Habits and similar species: A very easy bird to find due to its striking flight and noisy calls. May gather in very large flocks in winter, sometimes with smaller numbers of Golden Plover. Feeds on a variety of soil invertebrates; often active at night. Sociable Plover lacks crest but has dark crown and is grey-brown above with a dark underside in summer.

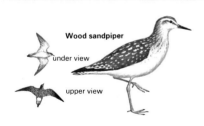

Wood sandpiper

under view

upper view

WOOD SANDPIPER
Tringa glareola L23cm
Characteristics: A medium-sized wader with a straight bill and long yellowish legs. The brownish upperparts are mottled and the underside is white. In flight the wings look distinctly pale beneath and have paler patches on the forewings above, unlike the dark upper and underwings in the Green Sandpiper. The rump is pale and the tail shows faint barring; the legs extend noticeably further beyond the tail in flight than in other sandpipers. Flight calls include a triple-note 'wee-wee-wee' and 'chiff-iff-iff' and the song is a more musical trilling version of the calls, reminiscent of Redshank.

Distribution and habitat: Very scarce breeding bird in northern Britain, more widespread in far northern Europe and Scandinavia. Nests on ground by swampy pools but may use an abandoned nest in a tree. More familiar as passage migrant in Britain in autumn.

Habits and similar species: Feeds on a wide range of invertebrates, including insects, caught by the margins of freshwater pools. If flushed has towering escape flight. Common Sandpiper has shorter legs, lacks white rump and shows broad pale wing bar in flight. Green Sandpiper has darker wings with no wing bar and has more shrill 'weet-a-weet' alarm note.

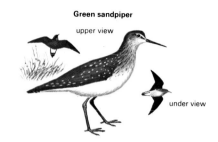

Green sandpiper
upper view

under view

Distribution and habitat: Breeds in boggy, wooded areas in northern Europe and Scandinavia, building its nest inside an

abandoned nest in a tree. The newly hatched young have to drop from the tree to the ground before they can feed. Migrates south for the winter.

GREEN SANDPIPER
Tringa ochropus L23cm
Characteristics: A medium-sized wader with greenish legs and dark upperparts contrasting strongly with the white rump and barred tail when viewed in flight. In good light the back is seen to be lightly speckled. The shrill 'weet-weet' or 'weet-a-weet' call is given when flushed and repeated several times; the towering flight and snipe-like habit of zig-zagging away to safety are good field characteristics. On the breeding grounds a trilling musical song is heard.

Habits and similar species: Overwinters in small flocks, sometimes singly, beside small freshwater pools, streams and watercress beds, usually avoiding reedbeds and larger marshes. Feeds on small invertebrates caught in shallow water. The Common Sandpiper is browner above with slightly shorter legs and stands horizontally with constantly bobbing tail, usually solitary in habits.

80

Canada goose

Distribution and habitat: Introduced into Britain from Canada; now the only black goose breeding south of the Arctic

in Europe. Spreading east into Europe and Scanadinavia. Occasional vagrants from N. America distinguished by smaller size and more solitary habits.

CANADA GOOSE
Branta canadensis L90-100cm
Characteristics: The largest of the 'black' geese and easily distinguished by its longer black neck, larger bill and white chin strap. The plumage is much browner than the Barnacle Goose and the slightly barred flanks give way to a pale underside. Canada Geese are very variable in size, with single small birds often being genuine vagrants from North America. The loud honking di-syllabic call is often heard as birds fly in to roost at night, or off to feed at dawn. During the mating season there is a great deal of calling.

Habits and similar species: Feeds on grasses and seeds, often on agricultural land, sometimes on aquatic vegetation. Nests in colonies near freshwater. Usually remains inland in winter, but may move to coastal marshes. Adult Brent Goose has small white patch on neck but is smaller and much darker and almost exclusively coastal. Barnacle Goose has white face, shorter black neck and dark upperparts.

Distribution and habitat:

Introduced into Britain from China and now naturalised by lakes and rivers with wooded margins. Nests in holes in waterside trees, using female's down as a lining.

	JAN	FEB	MAR	APR	MAY	JUN	JULY	AUG	SEPT	OCT	NOV	DEC
PRESENT												
BREEDING												
SONG												

MANDARIN DUCK
Aix galericulata L43cm

Characteristics: The male is a striking bird with conspicuous orange-chestnut projections on the wings and bright orange patches on the cheeks. The brown crest extends beyond the nape down on to the back. The female is mostly grey-brown with mottled flanks, a white eye-ring with a white stripe extending back along the head and a blue hindwing.

Habits and similar species: Feeds on leaves and seeds of aquatic and marginal plants, and takes some insects. Wood Duck, *Aix sponsa*, is slightly larger (L47cm). Drake lacks wing projections and has glossy green head with sleek crest and spotted chestnut breast. Duck has more striking teardrop-shaped eye ring and green tinge on back of crown.

81

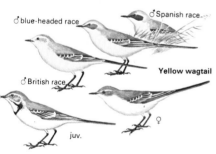

YELLOW WAGTAIL
Motacilla flava L16.5cm

Characteristics: Many races exist, each confined to a distinct geographical area, with different coloured heads evident in the males, but the British birds generally have a greenish-yellow head, a yellow throat and a yellow stripe above the eye. The upperparts are mostly greenish and the underside is a bright yellow. Females are similar to the males, but with a less intense yellow colour below. Juveniles are hard to distinguish from Pied or White Wagtails. Males sometimes sit on posts to sing trilling 'chip-chip-chip' song.

Distribution and habitat:

A common summer visitor to southern Britain, arriving in spring in large numbers before dispersing to wet meadows and grassy lake and river margins. Often roosts in reedbeds in large flocks before autumn migration, and may occur on coasts.

	JAN	FEB	MAR	APR	MAY	JUN	JULY	AUG	SEPT	OCT	NOV	DEC
PRESENT												
BREEDING												
SONG												

Habits and similar species: Feeds on insects, some caught on the wing over low vegetation, and small seeds. Often associated with cattle, collecting insects disturbed by their feet. Grey Wagtail also has yellow underside, but has black bib and grey back with much longer tail. Citrine Wagtail has darker back, but bright yellow head and no eye-stripe.

Common sandpiper

COMMON SANDPIPER
Actitis hypoleucos L20cm

Characteristics: A small wader with mostly solitary habits. Often seen perched close to the water on a low stone constantly bobbing its head and tail. When disturbed does not tower away, but is more likely to make rapid horizontal flight on flickering wings low over the water to safety, giving its shrill 'twee-wee-wee' call. A circular display flight is performed by males over breeding sites with a more elaborate and longer version of the call forming its song. The broad white wing bars, white underparts and white sides to the tail and rump are good distinctions from other small sandpipers.

Distribution and habitat: A fairly common breeding bird beside stony rivers and lakes in northern Britain, Europe and Scandinavia. Sometimes also occurs by sheltered coastal bays and inlets. Moves to coastal marshes and estuaries in winter.

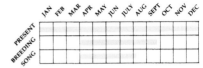

Habits and similar species: Feeds on small invertebrates, especially insects, caught at the edge of the water. Nests on the ground in a small scrape lined with vegetation. Green Sandpiper lacks the wing bar and has much darker wings above and below. Both Green and Wood Sandpipers have white rumps. Spotted Sandpiper is rare vagrant which has spotted breast in summer and dark-tipped bill.

imm.

Dipper

DIPPER
Cinclus cinclus L18cm

Characteristics: A striking bird of fast-flowing rivers, usually seen perched on a stone in the middle of the river constantly bobbing up and down. The white chest contrasts with the dark upperparts and dark chestnut belly; birds from northern and south-western Europe, sometimes called Black-bellied Dippers, have no chestnut below. Short tail is usually cocked up in a wren-like stance. Shrill song penetrates even the most raging of torrents and is often uttered from a stone near a waterfall.

Distribution and habitat: Confined mainly to upland regions in northern and western Britain and Europe where there are clear fast-flowing streams offering plenty of invertebrates. Nests behind waterfalls or under old bridges.

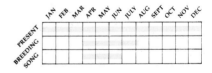

Habits and similar species: Swims well on the surface and underwater, and walks easily on submerged boulders in fast-flowing currents gripping with sharp claws. Feeds on aquatic invertebrates above and below the surface. May even walk below ice on partly frozen rivers. No other riverside bird has the ability to walk underwater as well as the Dipper.

Grey wagtail

Distribution and habitat: A fairly common resident beside fast-flowing rivers and streams in hilly districts, but also besides

weirs, mill-races and on watercress beds in lowland areas. May move to lower altitudes or into urban areas in winter.

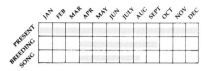

GREY WAGTAIL
Motacilla cinera L18cm

Characteristics: A very long-tailed wagtail with bluish-grey upperparts and a lemon-yellow underside. In the breeding season males have a black throat; females may have some spotting on the yellow throat. The yellow colouring is particularly bright near the base of the tail. The short 'tsee-tsee-tsee' song is sometimes given from a perch and sometimes in flight, although it is not often heard. A harsh 'ziz-iz' call is like the Pied Wagtail's but higher pitched.

Habits and similar species: Feeds on aquatic insects and other invertebrates, some caught from the ground and others chased in the air. May sometimes perch in quite tall trees unlike other wagtails. Usually nests in a crevice very close to the water, especially under stone bridges. Yellow Wagtail has shorter tail, greenish back and no black on chin.

83

WOODLANDS

Most of lowland Britain and Europe was once covered by mixed deciduous woodland. Much of this has now been cleared and what remains has nearly all been modified by man in some way. In a few places where ancient woodland remains, there is a predominance of old trees, a mixture of native shrub and understorey species and a variety of micro-habitats in the form of dead wood, small clearings, new growth and mature timber.

Woodlands like this are excellent places for birds as there is plenty of food for them and a good range of places to nest in. Woodlands which are managed by man for commercial reasons still support birds, but they often lack the variety of species found in ancient woodlands. Without dead timber there will be very few wood-boring beetles so woodpeckers will be less common. If there is little variety in the shrub layer there will be less for the seed eaters and insectivores to feed on. Nesting sites will be scarce in woods in which the trees are all of the same size and age, and lacking in holes, splits and damaged branches.

Commercial plantations, in which a single species (usually of an alien conifer) is planted to the exclusion of all else, are of far less value to birds than natural woodlands. They still have their own birdlife, however, and some species which specialise in feeding in conifers, such as Crossbills, have actually increased in certain areas because of the spread of commercial forestry. When these forests are first planted the young trees provide cover for ground-nesting birds like Hen Harriers and Nightjars, but as the trees reach maturity they are unable to live there and have to find new breeding sites.

Hedgerows are a substitute for woodlands in farming country and many woodland birds have adapted to feeding in different habitats, like parks and gardens, but as woodlands disappear their special birds will vanish with them.

A cock Pheasant at the edge of a foresry plantation.

85

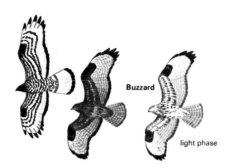

Buzzard

light phase

BUZZARD
Buteo buteo L50-56cm
Characteristics: A large bird of prey with predominantly brown plumage, although very pale individuals are not uncommon. Looks broad-winged in flight and has a short rounded tail which is barred and has a dark terminal band. Often sits on posts in the open and if disturbed flies off with slow strong wingbeats. Also seen circling high in the sky on slightly raised wings, using thermals in summer. Sometimes hovers briefly before diving down onto prey. Legs relatively short and featherless on the tarsi. Usual call is a plaintive, descending 'mee-ooo'.

Distribution and habitat: A widespread and sometimes common breeding bird in upland, wooded country and coasts.

Nests in large trees, also cliffs. May move to farmland in winter; summer visitor to most of Scandinavia. Very scarce in Ireland and eastern England.

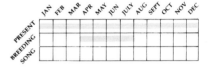

Habits and similar species: Feeds on a variety of small mammals, especially rabbits, small ground-feeding birds, invertebrates and carrion, often using a post as a look-out. Rough-legged Buzzard is a rare winter visitor with a greyer head, much darker carpal patches and a pale tail without barring but with one dark terminal band.

Honey buzzard

HONEY BUZZARD
Pernis apivorus L51-58cm
Characteristics: Very similar to Buzzard at first glance, especially when soaring, but when seen in outline the neck seems narrower with a smaller head and the tail seems longer. In gliding flight the wings look longer and less broad than Buzzard's, and if seen head on are seen to be held slightly depressed. Head of male is greyish with a yellow eye. Females have a browner head, but this is a very variable species. The tail shows a dark terminal band and two narrower dark bands near the base.

Distribution and habitat: A scarce breeding bird in Britain, confined to large forests in the south of England, but more widespread in Europe in open woodland. Migrates south in large numbers, with many being trapped and shot as they pass through Mediterranean countries.

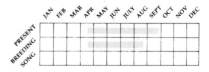

Habits and similar species: Feeds on larvae of wasps and bees which it digs out of their nests by scratching with its talons. Will also take lizards, frogs and small birds and mammals. May sit in tree for long periods watching bees return to their nest before attacking. Call is more shrill and shorter than Buzzard's. Compare Buzzard's larger head and bill, and brown, not yellow eye.

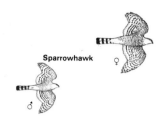

Sparrowhawk ♀

♂

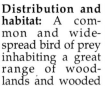

Distribution and habitat: A common and widespread bird of prey inhabiting a great range of woodlands and wooded country; usually breeds in woods, but may hunt outside woods along hedgerows or in gardens. Summer visitor in the northern part of its range.

SPARROWHAWK
Accipiter nisus L28-38cm

Characteristics: A small bird of prey with broad rounded wings and a long tail. The male is appreciably smaller than the female and his wings are more pointed. Both male and female have barred underparts, but the male's coloration is more rufous. By contrast, the male's back is grey-blue and the female's is dark brown. Both have noticeably long legs and talons used to capture small birds in flight. Soaring flight on outstretched wings is interspersed with three or four wing flaps; there is sometimes a plunging downwards dive with folded wings.

	JAN	FEB	MAR	APR	MAY	JUN	JULY	AUG	SEPT	OCT	NOV	DEC
PRESENT												
BREEDING												
SONG												

Habits and similar species: Presence may be indicated by 'plucking posts' where prey has been plucked before eating, leaving piles of feathers behind. Often sits concealed and then pursues small birds with a rapid dash; sometimes flies over or through hedgerows to surprise prey. Goshawk has similar outline but is much larger. Hobby also pursues small birds, but has much narrower and more pointed wings.

87

Goshawk

imm.

Distribution and habitat: A scarce breeding bird, formerly exterminated in Britain, but now found in scattered localities, possibly established through falconer's escapes. Prefers large areas of mixed mature woodland, but will hunt in the open over farmland.

GOSHAWK
Accipiter gentilis L50-60cm

Characteristics: Like an extra-large Sparrowhawk, the size of a Buzzard, but with shorter wings and a longer tail. The sexes are very alike in colouring, but the male is smaller than the female. Male can be separated from similar-sized female Sparrowhawk by heavier-looking body and more powerful wing-beats. Both sexes have white eye-stripes and white under-tail coverts. The call is a louder and harsher version of the Sparrowhawk's 'kek kek kek'. When seen perched looks broad-bodied and bulky.

	JAN	FEB	MAR	APR	MAY	JUN	JULY	AUG	SEPT	OCT	NOV	DEC
PRESENT												
BREEDING												
SONG												

Habits and similar species: Able to fly with great agility through woodland in pursuit of prey, manoeuvring easily through dense cover. Also flies at speed over trees and open ground. Usually takes birds from thrush to Wood Pigeon size, but will also take prey as large as Pheasant. Buzzard is similar size and lives in wooded country, but has longer and broader wings and shorter more rounded tail.

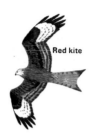

Red kite

RED KITE
Milvus milvus L60-65cm

Characteristics: The only large bird of prey with a deeply forked tail. The tail has rich rufous colourings and the rest of the plumage is more rufous than the similar-sized Buzzard. Adults have a pale head and pale eye, juveniles have more uniform colouring with pale streaking on the breast. In flight the wings show large white panels below and are often held at a sharp angle whilst gliding, but normal flight is quite buoyant and harrier-like. The tail is continuously twisted and turned in flight. A shrill mewing, rather thin buzzard-like call is also given in flight.

Black kite

BLACK KITE
Milvus migrans L56cm

Characteristics: A large bird of prey with a forked tail, but this is not always easy to see in flight, as it can look almost square-ended. Rather like a dark Buzzard, but in flight does not soar as much and flaps wings more often, holding them at a slight backwards angle. When gliding, the wings are held level and the tail is twisted from side to side. A gregarious bird and quite vocal giving frequent whinnying calls, which sound gull-like at times.

Distribution and habitat: A very scarce and local breeding bird in Britain. Recently been reintroduced to some areas. More widespread in central and southern Europe, nesting in wooded areas, hilly country and open rough country with scattered trees.

Habits and similar species: Feeds on a variety of small birds and mammals, but takes a great deal of carrion and may frequent slaughterhouses and refuse tips. Much persecuted by hunters and gamekeepers and often killed by poison baits. Black Kite also has forked tail, but it is less deeply indented.

Distribution and habitat: Only a rare vagrant to Britain. Widespread summer visitor in Europe migrating across the Bosphorous in great numbers. Nests in a wide range of habitats, but not densely wooded country. Often near water and sometimes near towns.

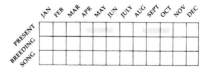

Habits and similar species: Takes a great range of small birds, mammals and fish, often scavenging along the edge of lakes and on refuse tips, sometimes in large flocks. One of the most numerous birds of prey in the world. Red Kite has more deeply forked tail and is much more rufous.

Pheasant

Distribution and habitat: Common and widespread. Mainly found in wooded areas in lowland and hilly regions, but may feed in open and may occur in dense scrub, reed beds or riverine woods. Nests on the ground in dense cover but roosts in trees.

PHEASANT
Phasianus colchicus L53-89cm
Characteristics: A very common game-bird now successfully naturalised over a huge area, and still escaping to the wild from game farms. Males larger than females with longer tails and more striking coloration. Males can be very variable with some having complete white collar, others none at all; some show white wing patches, and some may be melanistic or flavistic birds. Females more uniform, but paler colours are sometimes seen.

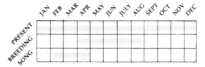

Habits and similar species: Reared in vast numbers for shooting. Feeds on invertebrates and plants on woodland floor. Male has variety of clucking, hen-like calls used when group of females are feeding around him and strident crow given in display. Loud roost call heard at dusk as birds fly up to branches. Golden Pheasant has rich scarlet underside and large expanse of gold on rump and crown.

89

Woodcock

Distribution and habitat: A widespread breeding bird over most of Britain and Europe. Prefers damp mixed woodlands with rides and clearings and plenty of ground cover. In the north is confined to birch woods; migrates south and west for the winter, flying at night.

WOODCOCK
Scolopax rusticola L36cm
Characteristics: An unusual wading bird with nocturnal and secretive habits. Rarely seen on the ground, but looks like small plump game-bird or large snipe. Bill very long and legs short with plumage which matches the leaf-litter of the woodland floor making it very difficult to observe. Male's evening display flight over breeding ground, known as 'roding', best way to see bird; usually flies at dusk over woodland rides and clearings with bill held downwards uttering curious croaking calls and a shrill 'tsi-wick'.

Habits and similar species: Feeds on soil invertebrates, especially earth-worms, collected from the woodland floor, and is most active at night. If flushed during the day flies low and quickly. Nests on ground in a shallow scrape lined with dead leaves. Snipe is smaller, slimmer, has longer bill and is confined to more open wetter habitats. Water Rail sometimes seen in open, but flanks barred and bill is shorter.

Stock dove

STOCK DOVE
Columba oenas L33cm

Characteristics: A slim dark grey pigeon lacking any conspicuous areas of white on its plumage. The wings have dark tips and there are two short dark wing bars. In flight appears to be slimmer and faster than the Wood Pigeon with which it often mixes. On its own, and when making its circular display flight, the whistling wing noises may be heard. The usual call is a monotonous cooing 'oo-look oo-look' repeated many times.

Distribution and habitat: A widespread and common breeding bird over most of Britain and Europe; absent from the far north. Found in parks, woodland edges, farm land and coastal areas. Usually nests in tree holes, but also uses cliffs and buildings.

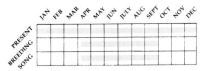

Habits and similar species: Feeds on leaves and seeds, usually collected from the ground and will feed in mixed flocks with other pigeons, especially on open farmland. Rock Dove has white rump and more striking black wing bars. Wood Pigeon is larger with white patches on wings. Collared Dove has more buff coloration with partial dark collar.

Wood pigeon

imm.

WOOD PIGEON
Columba palumbus L41cm

Characteristics: A large plump pigeon with mostly grey plumage, but large white patches on sides of neck and transverse white wing bars. When taking off wings make loud clapping noise. Outside breeding season may be found in very large flocks, sometimes associated with other species. The soothing 'oo-ooo-ooo-oo-oo' call is repeated three or four times and then ends with a final 'oo'.

Distribution and habitat: A very common and widespread breeding bird found in a great variety of habitats. Most usual nesting site is in a tree in woodland, but also nests in parks, making a precarious see-through platform of twigs.

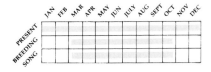

Habits and similar species: Feeds on plant material, especially leaves, seeds, including cereals, and buds. Solitary, or in small groups in breeding season; feeds in large flocks in winter. Stock Dove is smaller and lacks white markings; Rock Dove has white rump with black wing bars. Feral Pigeon more variable but closest in appearance to Rock Dove. May mix with Wood Pigeon in towns but not farmland.

Turtle dove

imm.

TURTLE DOVE
Streptopelia turtur L27cm
Characteristics: A small dark dove with mottled brownish upperparts and black and white patches on the sides of the neck. In flight the tail appears black with a conspicuous white edge above and below. Sometimes difficult to see but presence noted by its continuous purring 'turrr turrr' call.

Distribution and habitat: Widespread summer visitor. Prefers thick hedgerows, scrub and open woodland near farmland. Usually nests in a dense bush, but feeds on ground in the open, especially on flowers and seeds of Fumitory.

	JAN	FEB	MAR	APR	MAY	JUN	JULY	AUG	SEPT	OCT	NOV	DEC
PRESENT												
BREEDING												
SONG												

Habits and similar species: A shy and secretive bird, flying off a long way when flushed as it is greatly persecuted in the Mediterranean countries which it passes through on spring and autumn migration. Usually seen best on migration as it is more secretive on its breeding grounds. Collared Dove has plainer and paler colourings above and a black half collar.

91

Tawny owl

rufous phase   grey phase

TAWNY OWL
Strix aluco L38cm
Characteristics: Commonest of the medium-sized brown owls and very nocturnal. Most easily detected during the day by the mobbing calls of small birds. Plumage is a dark mottled brown and face is brown with large black eyes. In flight it appears plump with short rounded wings; able to fly through dense woodland on silent wings. A long, tremulous hoot is a frequently heard call; also a sharper 'kewick' call, often given by young birds.

Distribution and habitat: Common and widespread over most of Britain; not far north or Ireland. Widespread in Europe and southern Scandinavia. Usually nests in tree holes, but will use boxes, in open woodlands, parks, mature gardens, even city centres with trees.

	JAN	FEB	MAR	APR	MAY	JUN	JULY	AUG	SEPT	OCT	NOV	DEC
PRESENT												
BREEDING												
SONG												

Habits and similar species: Catches small mammals and birds at night, often in total darkness, using its acute hearing to locate them. Coughs up pellets of fur and bones, the remains of prey, found below habitual roosts. Long-eared Owl also brown, but slimmer, long ear tufts and orange eyes. Short-eared Owl more diurnal, preferring open country; has paler plumage, short ear-tufts and yellow eyes.

Nightingale

NIGHTINGALE
Luscinia megarhynchos L16.5cm
Characteristics: A secretive woodland bird most often detected by its loud, melodious song. If glimpsed in the preferred thick cover, it gives the impression of a slim thrush with plain brown unmarked plumage and rufous tail. Juveniles look more like outsize Robins. Song is as likely to be heard by day as by night, and is usually delivered from dense cover. It contains many melodious phrases and also some harsher notes. A number of loud 'chack chack' calls are interspersed with musical phrases and a shrill crescendo based on 'pioo pioo pioo'; unlike any other woodland bird's song.

92

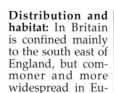

Distribution and habitat: In Britain is confined mainly to the south east of England, but commoner and more widespread in Europe. Usually found in broad-leaved woodland, coppices, thickets and dense hedgerows. Many trapped on migration through the Mediterranean.

Habits and similar species: A skulking woodland bird which nests and feeds in dense cover. Woodland invertebrates, especially insects, are the main food species, but tiny fruits and berries are sometimes taken. Thrush Nightingale, confined mainly to eastern Europe and Russia, is darker above and lacks rufous tail, and has slightly speckled breast, although these features are only detectable at close range.

Black woodpecker

BLACK WOODPECKER
Dryocopus martius L46cm
Characteristics: A very large woodpecker with all-black plumage. The male is the only black land-bird with a red crest; females are browner and have a much smaller patch of red on the nape. Holds its neck at a very stiff angle, unlike any other woodpecker. Produces a loud fluty far-carrying call.

Distribution and habitat: Not found in Britain or extreme western Europe. Confined mainly to mature coniferous forests and some mixed woodlands in central and northern Europe. Nests in a hole bored in a tree and does not use any nesting material.

Habits and similar species: Flies from tree to tree with a markedly uneven flight pattern, sometimes uttering a shrill 'krri krri krri' flight call. Uses strong ivory-coloured bill to find insects below bark and in rotten wood, especially old stumps, and sometimes leaves very large craters. In flight may be confused with similar sized crow, but neck is longer and tail is longer, narrower and more pointed.

imm.   Green woodpecker

♂

GREEN WOODPECKER
Picus viridus L32cm
Characteristics: A large woodpecker with mostly green plumage and a conspicuously yellow rump seen well in flight. Both male and female have a red crown and black moustachial stripes, but male has red moustachial stripes as well. Juveniles are paler but have darker specklings. In spring makes a loud and far-carrying 'plu-plu-plu' call, but throughout the year the yelping, laughing call is heard, especially if birds are disturbed whilst feeding on the ground.

Distribution and habitat: A common and widespread breeding bird over most of Britain and Europe, but absent from northern Scotland and Ireland. Prefers open woodland and parkland where there is plenty of grassland in which it can find ants, although it also feeds in trees.

Habits and similar species: Often seen on ground using its long sticky tongue to catch ants; the green helps camouflage it in grassland. The Grey-headed Woodpecker is smaller (L25cm) with similar green coloration, but has a distinctly grey head and very thin black moustachial stripes. Only males have red on the forehead. The call is similar to Green Woodpecker's but slower and more melodious.

GREAT SPOTTED WOODPECKER
Dendrocopus major L23cm
Characteristics: Commonest black and white woodpecker with large white wing patches, red under-tail coverts. Juveniles have red crown, females have all-black head, males have tiny red nape patch. Drums in one second bursts and gives a sharp 'chick' call.

Distribution and habitat: A common breeding bird over most of Britain and Europe, but absent from Ireland. Breeds in both coniferous and broad-leaved woodlands, parks, mature gardens as well as orchards. Often visits bird tables in winter.

Habits and similar species: It has a varied diet, but in winter feeds on seeds in particular. May wedge cones into bark crevices to extract the seeds. Middle Spotted Woodpecker slightly smaller, has red crown, white face and rose-coloured under-tail coverts; absent from Britain. White-backed Woodpecker has conspicuous white patch on lower back, no white wing patch. Confined to central and eastern Europe.

Lesser spotted
woodpecker

LESSER SPOTTED WOODPECKER
Dendrocopus minor L14.5cm
Characteristics: Smallest woodpecker, little larger than a Great Tit, with a distinctive barred appearance and no red under tail coverts. Males have a red crown, females lack any red markings. Usual call is a shrill 'pee-pee-pee', rather like Nuthatch. Drums frequently in spring in bursts of about two seconds, quieter than Great Spotted.

Distribution and habitat: Fairly common in open mixed woodland and areas with scattered trees such as parkland, mature gardens and orchards. Absent from northern Britain and Ireland. Nests in tree holes, often on underside of large branches.

Habits and similar species: May visit orchards, reed-beds and riverside woodlands in winter, feeding mainly on insects, but sometimes takes seeds. If seen in the open its flight is deeply undulating, and upperparts can look very white. Three-toed Woodpecker is larger (L22cm) and has mostly black wings with only slight barring. Males have a yellow crown and both sexes lack any red.

Marsh tit

MARSH TIT
Parus palustris L11.5cm
Characteristics: A small agile woodland bird with a shiny black crown, nape and chin. Best separated from almost identical Willow Tit by call; usually utters an explosive 'pitchou' and a harsh 'tchay', and sometimes makes a scolding 'chick-a-dee-dee-dee'. Its song is a sweeter sounding 'shippi-shippi-shippi'. In good light the glossy head may show up, and the lack of any pale wing panel may be evident.

Distribution and habitat: A common breeding bird over a wide area, but absent from northern Britain and Ireland. Prefers mixed broad-leaved woodland, dense hedgerows and overgrown gardens; rarely found in marshes; shows no particular preference for damper woodlands.

Habits and similar species: Usually found in ones or twos, and does not often mix with flocks of other tits. Collects seeds in winter and makes hoards low down in undergrowth; often makes repeated visits to bird feeders to collect its favourite seeds. Nests in holes in stumps, often very low down, but will use nest boxes. Willow Tit has sooty black crown and pale wing panel, and much harsher calls.

Willow tit

WILLOW TIT
Parus montanus L11.5cm
Characteristics: Very similar to Marsh Tit, but has sooty black crown and a pale panel on the wings; flanks may appear to be more buff-coloured than Marsh Tit. If seen together, Willow Tit has a larger head and thicker neck and area of black seems to be more diffuse at margins. Calls are easiest method of identification; Willow Tit makes a harsher and more nasal sounding 'tee tee chay chay' with the emphasis on the last two syllables which are longer. The song is a sweeter, warbler-like 'tyu-tyu-tyu' and is not often heard.

Distribution and habitat: A common breeding bird in coniferous and broad-leaved woodland; shows no preference for willows. Nests in holes excavated in rotten stumps by the female; will only use nesting boxes if filled with wood chips which female can remove herself.

Habits and similar species: Feeds on insects and seeds, often mixing with other species of tits in roving flocks in winter. More solitary in breeding season. Coal Tit has black crown with white nape patch. Crested Tit has similar calls, but larger black bib and collar, and paler speckled crown with distinct crest.

Treecreeper

TREECREEPER
Certhia familiaris L12.5cm
Characteristics: A small brown-speckled woodland bird with the unusual habit of climbing up tree trunks in a spiral fashion. The legs are very short and the toes are long with sharp claws which help the bird to grip onto bark. More often heard than seen, and makes a thin, slightly trilling 'srreee srreee' call. Its song is a quiet, silvery collection of short calls ending with a slight flourish.

Distribution and habitat: Common and widespread breeding bird found in a variety of woodlands; mature coniferous and broad-leaved woods preferred. Found at high altitude in coniferous woodlands in southern Europe where it overlaps with Short-toed Treecreeper.

Habits and similar species: Regularly runs up trees like a small mouse; usually spirals up the tree and then flies down to the base of the next tree before spiralling up again. Very rarely may be seen on a wall; sometimes gives a bat-like display flight. Nests under loose bark or in crevices. Short-toed Treecreeper very similar, but not found in Britain. Wren may perch on tree trunk, but does not run up bark.

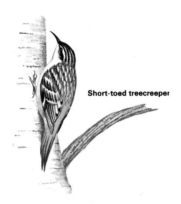

Short-toed treecreeper

SHORT-TOED TREECREEPER
Certhia brachydactyla L12.5cm
Characteristics: Hard to separate from Treecreeper, but flanks are browner, upperparts are very slightly darker and slightly more speckled. Supercilium is less clearly defined and rump lacks the rusty tinge. Bill is slightly longer, and in the hand the hind claw can be seen to be shorter. These features are difficult to observe in the field; the two species rarely overlap so the range aids identification. Calls shorter and higher than Treecreeper's.

Distribution and habitat: Where the two species overlap Short-toed is confined to lower altitude broad-leaved woodland, and in the southernmost part of its range is found in drier mature coniferous woodland. Found in Channel Islands but doubtfully in Britain.

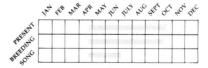

	JAN	FEB	MAR	APR	MAY	JUN	JULY	AUG	SEPT	OCT	NOV	DEC
PRESENT												
BREEDING												
SONG												

Habits and similar species: Like Treecreeper, catches insects on tree bark. Makes nest behind flaking bark, sometimes low down. Uses fine mosses and grasses as a lining. Usually solitary, feeding independently of other woodland birds.

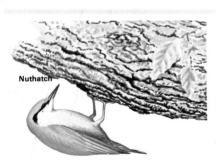

Nuthatch

NUTHATCH
Sitta europaea L14cm
Characteristics: A small tree-climbing bird with the unusual ability to run down tree trunks as well as up them. Although woodpecker-like in habits, the compact body, short tail and powerful pointed bill make it an easy bird to recognise in profile. The steely blue upperparts, orange-buff underside and bold black stripe through the eye also help separate the nuthatch from the woodpeckers. A very vocal bird with a variety of loud and ringing calls, and an equally loud and musical song, usually a variant of 'wee-u, wee-u, wee-u'.

Distribution and habitat: Common over southern Britain, Europe and Scandinavia. Absent from Ireland. Always found in wooded areas, usually mature mixed woodland, but also lives in parkland, orchards and mature gardens where it may be a regular visitor to bird tables.

	JAN	FEB	MAR	APR	MAY	JUN	JULY	AUG	SEPT	OCT	NOV	DEC
PRESENT												
BREEDING												
SONG												

Habits and similar species: Catches insects in bark crevices and takes a variety of seeds and nuts. Hard seeds are wedged in a bark crevice before being chiselled with the bill. Feeds with flocks of tits in winter and soon learns to exploit bird tables. The nest is made in a tree hole which is plastered with mud leaving a hole only just large enough for the bird to enter.

Wryneck

Distribution and habitat: A very rare summer visitor to Britain, probably extinct in the south, but now colonising north-east

Scotland. Commoner in Europe and Scandinavia, nesting in tree holes, and sometimes nesting boxes, in orchards, mature gardens and open woodlands.

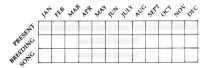

WRYNECK
Jynx torquilla L16.5cm

Characteristics: Although closely related to woodpeckers does not resemble them, having much shorter bill, longer tail, and far more cryptic markings. Mottled grey-brown upperparts resemble lichen-covered tree-trunks; the underside is brown and barred. A difficult bird to see when it is not moving, it is usually noticed by its shrill, nuthatch-like calls; sometimes a harsher version of the call is given, sounding like a distant Kestrel.

Habits and similar species: Feeds on insects, mainly caught on the ground, and is very fond of ants. Hops along the ground with its tail raised. Is able to make strange twisting snake-like movements with its neck, hence old country name of 'Snake Bird'. Flies with a less undulating flight than other woodpeckers and is more likely to fly through thick cover. Nests in holes in trees and will use boxes.

97

Woodlark

Distribution and habitat: A local breeding bird in southern Britain, usually in open woodland, recently cleared plantations

and woodland edges bordering heathlands. More widespread in Europe, found in a wider range of habitats from olive groves to alpine meadows.

WOODLARK
Lullula arborea L15cm

Characteristics: Similar to the more familiar Skylark, but has shorter slightly darker tail with no white border; in flight it has a bat-like appearance. The short crest is difficult to see in the field. Two buff-coloured eye-stripes extend beyond the eye to meet on the nape and the leading edge of the wing has a black and white patch marking the position of the 'wrist'. The beautiful, fluty song is a descending scale, increasing in speed and volume.

Habits and similar species: An easily overlooked bird which spends much of its time feeding on the ground, but when it is singing it is more obvious. The song may be delivered from a perch or from its high song flight very early in the morning and late in the evening. Skylark has a longer tail with white borders and a more powerful song delivered from its ascending song flight, never from a perch.

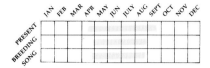

Golden oriole

GOLDEN ORIOLE
Oriolus oriolus L24cm

Characteristics: Despite the bright yellow and black coloration of the male, a very difficult bird to see as it spends most of its time high up in the tree canopy. Usually detected by its rich and musical song; a number of variations on 'weela wee-oo'. Both sexes make a variety of squealing cat-like calls, sometimes sounding like a Jay. Females and young males are greenish above with very dark primaries and a streaked underside.

Distribution and habitat: A very scarce summer visitor to Britain, with a few breeding pairs. Prefers broad-leaved woodland, especially poplar plantations, more open wooded areas, large mature parks and gardens. Nest of woven grasses is far out on a branch.

	JAN	FEB	MAR	APR	MAY	JUN	JULY	AUG	SEPT	OCT	NOV	DEC
PRESENT												
BREEDING												
SONG												

Habits and similar species: Catches insects and collects fruits high up in the canopy. When seen in flight, looks rather woodpecker-like, but flight is slightly less undulating. Females and juveniles may be confused with Green Woodpecker, but bill is shorter and there is no red in the plumage; unlike woodpeckers, orioles never crouch on tree-trunks or large branches.

WOOD WARBLER
Phylloscopus sibilatrix L12.5cm

Characteristics: A large leaf warbler with an obviously yellow breast contrasting with its white underside. The upperparts are greenish and there is a distinct yellow eye-stripe and a sad-sounding, bullfinch-like 'dee-u dee-u' call but also has a characteristic accelerating song, likened to a coin spinning on plate and finally settling. May give song from short song-flights in the canopy or from open perch.

Distribution and habitat: A common and widespread summer visitor over much of Britain, excluding Ireland. Common and widespread in Europe in summer. Prefers mature woodlands with a thin understorey and little ground cover, such as mature beech woods.

	JAN	FEB	MAR	APR	MAY	JUN	JULY	AUG	SEPT	OCT	NOV	DEC
PRESENT												
BREEDING												
SONG												

Habits and similar species: Catches insects in the leaf canopy and nearer the ground, sometimes by making short flights after them. Nests on the ground, making a domed nest of grasses and small leaves. Bonelli's Warbler is slightly smaller (11.5.cm) and greyer on the head and back, and lacks the yellow eye-stripe and breast; a very unusual vagrant in Britain, confined mainly to southern Europe.

Spotted flycatcher

imm.

SPOTTED FLYCATCHER
Muscicapa striata L14cm
Characteristics: A small grey-brown bird with darker streaks on both the head and the breast; only juvenile birds can really be described as spotted. The sexes are alike. Habitually sits on a prominent perch in an upright posture. Makes a thin 'tzee' call, sometimes followed by a quieter 'chuck'. The song is a sequence of five or six rather scratchy notes, given from the perch.

Distribution and habitat: A common summer visitor to Britain and Europe; found in a great range of wooded and more open habitats, but it prefers areas where it can perch near a clearing, perhaps a small garden, and look out for flying insects.

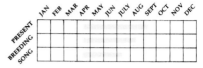

Habits and similar species: Makes short forays out from its perch to catch flying insects. Nests in holes, ivy-covered trunks, open nest-boxes and ledges, and sometimes uses old nest of other species. Female Pied Flycatcher is similar but lacks any streaks or spots. Female Red-breasted Flycatcher also lacks spots and has more buff-coloured breast.

99

Pied flycatcher

♀

♂

PIED FLYCATCHER
Ficedula hypoleuca L13cm
Characteristics: The male in breeding plumage is a striking black and white bird, and the only small bird of this coloration which regularly catches flies. Females are a more uniform greyish-brown above and males in winter are similar; they can be distinguished out of breeding plumage by a small white forehead patch. Juveniles are similar to females but have pale spots above and slight mottling below. Song is pleasant and rhythmic.

Distribution and habitat: A common summer visitor to northern and western Britain, and northern and central Europe. In Britain it is mainly found in mature deciduous woodland, often in hilly country; also occurs in coniferous woodland in Europe.

Habits and similar species: Sits on a prominent perch from which it makes dashing flights in pursuit of insects. Regularly uses hole-fronted nesting boxes; populations have increased dramatically where these have been provided. Collared Flycatcher very similar but male has complete white collar, white rump and more white on wings and forehead. Females and juveniles almost identical, but slightly greyer.

Redstart

REDSTART
Phoenicurus phoenicurus L14cm
Characteristics: The male is striking in breeding plumage with a bold black throat contrasting with a fiery red tail and underside. Upperparts are ashy-grey with a white forehead separating the grey crown from the black face. The female is much more subdued by comparison being mostly brownish above and paler below, but with a red tail like the male. In autumn the male has far less striking colours as the feathers develop brown edges, but in all plumages the tail remains red. When perched the tail is seen to be constantly quivering, a habit shared only with the Black Redstart. Song is short and mournful with a final quiet trill.

100

Tree pipit

song flights

TREE PIPIT
Anthus trivialis L15cm
Characteristics: A small, slender bird with a long tail and a fine pointed bill. The upperparts are brownish and streaked, although the rump is mostly unstreaked and the underside has a faint yellowish tinge, and a white belly. In good light the legs show a pink tinge. Usual call is a nasal-sounding 'speez'. When alarmed a slow and persistent 'sit sit sit' is uttered. Song sometimes delivered from a tree-top, but usually from a short song flight which itself may start from a tree-top song post. In this flight it launches itself and descends on stiffly held wings. It is quite a loud song consisting of a repetition of a series of short notes, some at slow tempo and some faster.

Distribution and habitat: A fairly common summer visitor to Britain and Europe. Prefers mature open woodlands

and hilly country with scattered mature trees. May also inhabit large old gardens and parks and even remote northern birch woods.

Habits and similar species: Feeds mainly on insects and small invertebrates, sometimes making short flights to catch them like a flycatcher. Nests in tree holes and readily uses boxes. Male Black Redstart has all black plumage apart from red tail. Male Stonechat has black head and white collar and dark tail, and is far less likely to be seen in woods.

Distribution and habitat: A common summer visitor to open wooded habitats, bushy heathlands, new forestry plantations with suitable song posts,

and forest edges. On migration may turn up in more varied habitats. It is present over most of Britain and Europe but not Ireland.

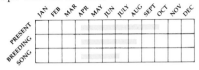

Habits and similar species: Feeds on insects and small seeds collected on the ground. Makes short dashes in pursuit of active insects. Nests in a hollow or beneath grass tussock using woven grass and animal hair. Meadow Pipit is very similar but has more olive-coloured upperparts and less yellow below. Rock Pipit is more coastal and has darker colouring.

Dunnock

DUNNOCK
Prunella modularis L15cm

Characteristics: A secretive and often skulking small bird with brown and grey colourings. Usually easier to hear than see as it makes its high-pitched 'tseep' call note. Although similar to a female House Sparrow at first glance, hence other English name of Hedge Sparrow, the thin insectivores bill, grey head and underparts and streaked flanks distinguish it from seed-eating sparrows. The song is a somewhat half-hearted warble, rather like a distant and flat Robin. When singing, the Dunnock sits out in a fairly exposed position, contrary to its usual habits.

Distribution and habitat: A very common resident, found over a wide area and in many different habitats, but it is commonest in bushy places where there is plenty of cover, such as woodland edges and rides, mature gardens and parks, and hedgerows.

Habits and similar species: Feeds mainly on insects but will take small seeds and visits bird feeding tables in winter. Normally remains in dense cover and is a difficult bird to census as it nests deep inside bushes. Alpine Accentor is larger (L18cm) and more strikingly marked with a black and white spotted throat and rufous flanks; confined to rocky mountain slopes, but comes lower in winter.

101

Grasshopper warbler

GRASSHOPPER WARBLER
Locustella naevia L13cm

Characteristics: An extremely difficult bird to see, although its presence is easy to detect by its characteristic prolonged song which sounds like an angler's reel being wound rapidly. It is delivered from thick cover and as the bird turns its head the volume changes; for this reason it is difficult to pinpoint the bird's position, even though the song is far-carrying. There is also a short 'chick' alarm note. The upperparts are dark olive-brown with darker streaks and the underside is paler without streaks.

Distribution and habitat: A widespread summer visitor to bushy and grassy habitats, often in young plantations, and in both wet and dry environments, where there is plenty of cover to conceal its ground-level nest. Absent from northern Scotland and Scandinavia.

Habits and similar species: Can run rapidly on the ground like a mouse through dense cover and makes short flitting flights when rounded tail is more obvious. Feeds on insects, but may take other invertebrates from the ground. Savi's Warbler is very similar but confined mainly to reedbeds and is very rare in Britain; it is larger and slightly less secretive.

Icterine warbler summer

imm.

ICTERINE WARBLER
Hippolais icterina L13.5cm
Characteristics: Like a large leaf warbler but with yellower colourings below and greenish-grey upperparts. There is only a very faint eye-stripe and the face has a plain appearance. The bill is broader and flatter than the typical leaf warbler's and has a pink tinge. In profile the head seems quite peaked. The song is a collection of both harsh and musical notes, including some mimicry and a characteristic 'gee-ah' sound, and there is a distinctive, melodious 'teet-lu-eet' call.

102

Distribution and habitat: Feeds and nests in cover, up to 4 metres above ground level, in woodland edges, rides, parks and shrubby gardens. A rare passage migrant to Britain, but a fairly common summer visitor in central and eastern Europe and southern Scandinavia.

Habits and similar species: Feeds mainly on insects, spiders and small invertebrates. Raises its crown when excited to give a peaked appearance. Melodious Warbler is very similar but is yellower below and has brown, rather than blue-grey legs. Its song is even more musical, and full of mimicry. A vagrant in Britain and replaces the Icterine Warbler in south-west Europe.

Whitethroat ♀

song flight

♂

WHITETHROAT
Sylvia communis L14cm
Characteristics: The male's excited chattering song delivered from a song perch makes this one of the easier warblers to see. The combination of grey head, white throat and reddish wing panels are unique to the Whitethroat. In the breeding season the male's white breast is suffused with pink and the head is greyer than the female's. Juveniles have a browner head. The song may also be given by the male during a short fluttering flight out from the usual song perch.

Distribution and habitat: A common summer visitor to a range of bushy and well-vegetated habitats, such as hedgerows, woodland edges and rides and large areas of brambles. Numbers reduced in recent years because of drought in African overwintering areas.

Habits and similar species: Feeds on insects, spiders and small fruits collected in low, dense vegetation. The nest is built of fine leaves and grasses and is placed low down in a bush. The Lesser Whitethroat is only slightly smaller (L13.5cm) but lacks the reddish wing panels, is greyer above and has more distinct dark 'ear' patches. Garden Warbler is same size, but lacks any distinctive features.

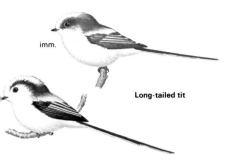

imm.

Long-tailed tit

LONG-TAILED TIT
Aegithalos caudatus L14cm
Characteristics: A small bird with a very long tail which makes up more than half the length of the body. The long tail and the black, white and pink colourings prevent confusion with other small woodland birds. Juveniles have blacker heads and lack the pink scapulars, but still have the long tail. Birds from northern Europe are much paler with an all-white head and less pink on the scapulars. As feeding flocks move through a wood they can be heard making their short 'tsrrrp' and 'tsee-seee' calls; the song is a quiet warbler-like trill.

Distribution and habitat: A common and widespread resident bird throughout most of Europe in woodlands, hedgerows, mature parks and gardens and other well-vegetated areas. In the north of its range numbers fluctuate when severe winters take their toll.

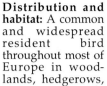

Habits and similar species: Usually found in small flocks of 5-15 birds, sometimes with other small woodland birds in winter. Flight looks weak as birds fly from tree to tree in undulating pattern. The nest is a beautiful domed construction of mosses, lichens, feathers and cobwebs, built inside a prickly bush like gorse or hawthorn, or high up against a trunk in honeysuckle or ivy.

103

imm.

Great tit

GREAT TIT
Parus major L14cm
Characteristics: A very common woodland bird with bold black and yellow coloration. The black chest band is wider in males. Juveniles are a paler yellow and have yellow rather than white cheeks. A very vocal bird with a great variety of calls; one of the most common is a persistent and strident 'teacher teacher teacher' with the accent on the first syllable. A Chaffinch-like 'chink chink' and a number of other shorter churring calls are also frequently given.

Distribution and habitat: A very common breeding bird in a wide variety of woodland habitats, also breeds in parks and gardens. Birds from the far north of Europe and Scandinavia migrate south in winter, many arriving on the east coast of England.

Habits and similar species: An agile and lively bird feeding on a variety of insects and seeds taken from ground level up to tree-canopy height; in summer takes mainly small caterpillars, but diet in autumn consists of many types of fruits and seeds. A frequent visitor to bird tables and very fond of peanuts. Coal Tit is smaller (L11.5cm), and lacks yellow coloration but still has black head and white face.

Blue tit

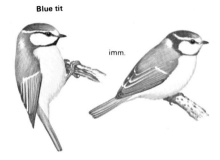

imm.

BLUE TIT
Parus caeruleus L11.5cm
Characteristics: The only small woodland bird with a blue crown. The white face is bordered with black and underside is yellow but lacks the black central band seen in the Great Tit. The upperparts are mainly green. Juvenile birds look much paler yellow and have no blue head or white face. Very vocal with a variety of churring and scolding calls based on a rapid 'tsee-tsee' or 'tsit tsit'. The song consists of two long notes followed by a rapid trill, but there are many variations on this.

104

Distribution and habitat: A very common resident bird over most of Britain and Europe, but absent from the far north and only 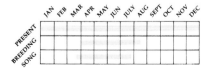 a summer visitor in the northern-most part of its range. Prefers deciduous woodlands and shrubby gardens, but occurs in many other wooded habitats.

	JAN	FEB	MAR	APR	MAY	JUN	JULY	AUG	SEPT	OCT	NOV	DEC
PRESENT												
BREEDING												
SONG												

Habits and similar species: An active and very agile bird, able to find food on the underside of branches by hanging upside down. Feeds on a variety of insects, invertebrates and small fruits and seeds. Frequent visitor to bird tables, often becoming the dominant species. Nests in natural holes in trees and walls, but readily takes to nesting boxes.

Wren

WREN
Troglodytes troglodytes L9.5cm
Characteristics: One of the smallest European birds. The small size, barred rusty-brown plumage and narrow cocked-up tail help separate it from other small birds such as warblers. It is highly active and has a rapid whirring flight. The song is surprisingly loud and melodious for such a small bird and is sometimes delivered from a prominent perch when the bird can be seen clearly, although it is usually given from thick cover. The song is a series of rapid trills and clear high notes, and usually ends with a flourish. There is also a harsh and repetitive scolding 'tic tic tic' call.

Distribution and habitat: A very common resident bird, inhabiting any area which offers thick cover and is found from sea level to high  moorland, including offshore islands. It is especially abundant in well-vegetated deciduous woodlands. Populations can be reduced in hard winters.

	JAN	FEB	MAR	APR	MAY	JUN	JULY	AUG	SEPT	OCT	NOV	DEC
PRESENT												
BREEDING												
SONG												

Habits and similar species: Feeds on woodland invertebrates, usually collected at ground level, but also feeds at higher level in bushy areas. Nests in thick vegetation, especially brambles, holes in banks and on ivy-covered tree-trunks. The nest is made from leaves and moss and has a domed top. Males build a series of nests and invite females to lay in them. Having attracted one mate he may go on to lure another.

Tree sparrow

TREE SPARROW
Passer montanus L14cm
Characteristics: Slightly smaller and slimmer than the House Sparrow with a chestnut crown. The sexes are identical, both having a smaller and neater black bib than the House Sparrow. The white cheek has a black patch on it, the rump is yellowish brown and the flanks have a warm buff colouration. Juveniles lack the buff coloration on the flanks and have a less distinct and paler black bib and cheek patch. The voice is similar to the House Sparrow but higher pitched and slightly less grating. There is a characteristic rapid 'chip chip' and a 'tec tec ' flight note.

Distribution and habitat: Occurs in a variety of open wooded habitats and agricultural land with hedgerows and scattered trees. May occur in small scattered colonies in open deciduous woodlands. Not usually present in suburbs or towns, but does occur in farmyards.

Habits and similar species: Feeds on seeds, especially cereals gleaned from fields, other plant material and some insects. Nests in holes in trees, and readily uses nest boxes if holes are large enough. The nest is a domed construction of grass and leaves lined with feathers. Spanish Sparrow is slightly larger (L14.5cm) and has more extensive and less distinct area of black on breast.

Jay

JAY
Garrulus glandarius L35cm
Characteristics: A common woodland bird but not always easy to see due to its wariness and nervous habits. Usually betrayed by its screeching calls and other far-carrying sounds. When seen in flight the white rump, white wing-patches and black tail are diagnostic. The blue wing patches are not a very obvious feature unless seen at close range. When angry the crest can be raised slightly. The wings look rounded in flight and the wingbeats seem rather laboured.

Distribution and habitat: Common over most of Britain and Europe except northern Scandinavia. Prefers mixed woodland, but occurs in a wide range of wooded habitats, including parks and gardens, and occasionally enters towns.

Habits and similar species: Feeds on a variety of seeds and fruits, especially acorns which it collects in large numbers and buries; it is the main agent of dispersal for oak seeds. Will also take invertebrates and sometimes small birds. Small groups of Jays on the wing in the open late in the year may be migrants fleeing harsh weather or a poor seed crop in their northern breeding areas.

HAWFINCH
Coccothraustes coccothraustes L18cm
Characteristics: A large plump finch with a massive solid bill. The short tail and stocky body make it look top-heavy when perched. In flight the short white-tipped tail, white wing patches and heavy bill are easily spotted features. Males have a blue-grey bill in the breeding season and slightly darker markings than female. Juveniles slightly spotted on the flanks and have a yellow throat. Usual calls are a 'tick' and a high-pitched whistling 'tsip'; feeble song not often heard.

Distribution and habitat: Prefers mature mixed woodlands, orchards, old gardens and hedgerows where there is a variety of seed-bearing trees. Widespread, but nowhere very common. Absent from the far north of Scotland, Ireland and Scandinavia.

Habits and similar species: Feeds on the hard seeds of cherries and hawthorn, and is particularly fond of Hornbeam. Even the toughest seeds can be cracked open using the massive bill. A migrant in the northern part of its range. The nest is a small cup of twigs and roots built at the end of a high branch. The Bullfinch has a smaller, stubbier bill and a striking black cap and white rump.

BRAMBLING
Fringilla montifringilla L14.5cm
Characteristics: Superficially like a Chaffinch, but orange-buff colourings, darker back and white rump are diagnostic. In summer males have a striking black hood; females are speckled brown above with grey cheeks. Various short nasal calls are produced and there is a quiet 'chec chec' flight call. The song is reminiscent of the Greenfinch's uninspiring and often repeated 'tseeeee'.

Distribution and habitat: Only a very rare breeding bird in northern Scotland, otherwise a winter visitor to Britain and Europe from its Scandinavian and far northern breeding grounds. Nests in remote birch forests but winters in deciduous woodlands, parks and farmlands.

Habits and similar species: A gregarious species sometimes migrating in vast flocks. Often associates with Chaffinches to form mixed feeding flocks in winter. Fond of beech mast, but will take various grains and seeds; feeds on insects in summer. Feeds mostly on the ground but when alarmed flocks suddenly take off for the safety of nearby trees. Bullfinch also has white rump but has black cap throughout the year.

107

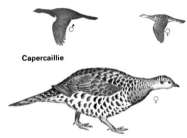

Capercaillie

CAPERCAILLIE
Tetrao urogallus L61-86cm
Characteristics: A very large game-bird, the male appreciably larger than the female, and looking like an enormous Black Grouse. Tail is long and broad and wings look relatively short in flight. Female may be mistaken for a female Black Grouse but is much larger and has a rufous breast and rounded tail. Males produce an extraordinary variety of croaking and popping calls, and when displaying the song is not bird-like; sounds likened to popping corks and gurgling liquids are followed by crashes made by scraping the wing quills along the ground.

Distribution and habitat: Re-introduced to Scotland, and now locally quite numerous. At home in mature coniferous forests, especially in hilly and mountainous country. Widespread in northern Europe and Scandinavia and in mountainous regions of southern Europe.

Habits and similar species: In winter feeds on pine needles from branches high up and makes a loud noise when leaving tree. Also takes buds, shoots and seeds of trees and shrubs. Males are polygamous and leave females to incubate and guard the chicks. Black Grouse similar but much smaller (male L35cm) and more likely to be seen in the open on moorland. Black Grouse may hybridise with Capercaillie.

Long-eared owl

LONG-EARED OWL
Asio otus L36cm

Characteristics: Only medium-sized brown owl with long ear tufts. Looks very slim when perched and when alarmed can stretch its body up to look even slimmer. Eyes are orange and the face looks more elongated than Tawny Owl's; in flight wings look longer and are almost white below. Not as vocal as the Tawny Owl; the male gives a soft 'oooh oooh oooh' call at a slow but regular rate and the female answers with a more nasal sounding 'paah'. A 'kwik kwik' alarm call is also given, and juveniles make a plaintive 'peeu'.

108

Distribution and habitat: A widespread breeding bird but nowhere very common. Often overlooked due to its very nocturnal and quiet habits. Northern breeding birds migrate south in winter, often congregating in small flocks in regular overwintering roosting sites.

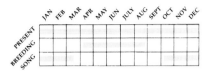

Habits and similar species: Catches a wide range of small mammals and birds in forests and more open wooded country. In winter may move to lowland areas, often roosting in dense scrub near water. Nests in abandoned Crows' nests using no nest material of its own. Short-eared Owl has much shorter ears, yellow eyes and is more diurnal. Tawny Owl is plumper, has dark eyes and no ear tufts.

Goldcrest

imm.

GOLDCREST
Regulus regulus L9cm

Characteristics: Alongside the Firecrest these are the two smallest European birds; the Goldcrest has a tiny black bill and a black-bordered crest, orange in the male and lemon-yellow in the female. The lowest of the two pale wing bars has a dark mark beside it. The very high pitched song sounds rather like a ground-glass stopper being twisted in a bottle, but has a definite rhythm. There is also a thin, short call note, sometimes lost amongst the calls of other small woodland birds like Treecreeper and Coal Tit.

Distribution and habitat: A very common breeding bird; more numerous in Britain in winter when resident population is augmented by migrants from further north and east. Prefers conifer woodlands, but occurs in many other wooded habitats such as mature gardens and parks.

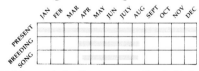

Habits and similar species: Feeds high in canopy on tiny insects, making fluttering dashes after prey. May leave coniferous woods to feed at lower level in winter, mixing with other small woodland birds. Firecrest has prominent black and white head markings. Pallas's Warbler is tiny leaf warbler from Asia with yellow crown stripe and eye stripes, no black on head, two yellow wing bars and yellow rump.

Firecrest

imm.

FIRECREST
Regulus ignicapillus L9cm
Characteristics: Similar in many ways to the Goldcrest, but has a striking black and white striped head pattern and a greenish-bronze patch on the side of the neck. The song is like a faster version of the Goldcrest's but is composed of more monosyllabic notes and accelerates towards the end. The 'zit zit' call sounds sharper than the Goldcrest's, although this is not always easy to hear, and it rises in pitch towards the end. There is sometimes a call similar to the Coal Tit's.

Distribution and habitat: A very scarce breeding bird in southern Britain, but seems to be increasing. Commoner in southern Europe and a summer visitor in central Europe. Most likely to be seen around the coast during autumn migration.

	JAN	FEB	MAR	APR	MAY	JUN	JULY	AUG	SEPT	OCT	NOV	DEC
PRESENT												
BREEDING												
SONG												

Habits and similar species: Found in similar habitats to Goldcrest, but not especially tied to conifers; occurs in parks and large gardens. Nests high up and far out on a branch making tiny cup of mosses, cobwebs and lichens lined with feathers. Catches insects on large trees but will come down to feed in shrubby areas. Yellow-browed Warbler slightly larger, has two yellow wing bars, and yellow eye-stripe.

Coal tit

imm.

COAL TIT
Parus ater L11cm
Characteristics: A small woodland bird with a black crown and bib, a white face and white nape patch, and two faint white wing bars. The underside has a pale buff tone, particularly on the flanks. Juveniles have a yellowish tinge to the white areas of the body. Like the Great Tit, there are many calls, but the 'tichaa tichaa' call is higher pitched and has the emphasis on the second syllable. A high-pitched 'tsee' or 'twee twee' call may cause some confusion with Goldcrest if the birds can not be seen.

Distribution and habitat: Mainly a bird of coniferous forests; also breeds in mixed deciduous woodland, parks and gardens. Common and widespread in suitable habitats, often migrating in vast numbers when Spruce trees in northern areas fail to produce a seed crop.

	JAN	FEB	MAR	APR	MAY	JUN	JULY	AUG	SEPT	OCT	NOV	DEC
PRESENT												
BREEDING												
SONG												

Habits and similar species: Feeds on seeds, especially conifer seeds, and insects in summer. Will visit bird tables and feed in mixed flocks with other woodland birds. Nests in holes, mainly in trees, but sometimes at very low level in banks or walls. Great Tit is larger and has yellow underparts. Both Marsh and Willow Tit have black crowns, but no white nape patch or wing bars.

Crested tit

CRESTED TIT
Parus cristatus L12cm

Characteristics: The only small woodland bird with a pronounced crest. Sometimes it is held flatter on to the head and is not so obvious, but the combination of white face with C-shaped black mark, speckled black and white head and lack of wing bars are useful features to separate this species from Coal Tit. The back is also browner than in most of the other tits. Makes a quiet 'si-si-si' call and a soft churring scold; the song is a more high-pitched trilling variation of two notes.

Distribution and habitat: Confined in Britain to mature conifer forests in Scotland, but is much more widespread in Europe, occurring in a greater variety of mature mixed woodlands, but usually associated with conifers. Very sedentary and not given to long migrations.

Habits and similar species: Feeds on seeds and small invertebrates, sometimes associating with Coal Tits, but more likely to be seen feeding near the ground. Nests in rotten stumps in holes excavated by the female; uses a lining of mosses and animal hair. Marsh and Willow Tit lack crests and have un-speckled black heads with unmarked white faces; both are less likely to occur in conifer forests.

110

Crossbill
♀
♂

CROSSBILL
Loxia curvirostra L16.5cm

Characteristics: At close range the curious crossed mandibles make this bird easy to identify, but at a distance they may not be so obvious. At longer range the large size, method of feeding on cones and the persistent 'chip chip' flight calls and contact notes are good identification features. The song is a combination of these calls and short trills. Sexes different with males showing the brightest colourings, being mostly red. Females are olive-green and juveniles are greyish and streaked.

Distribution and habitat: Confined to coniferous woodlands, but especially spruce forests. Numbers can vary from year to year according to the food supply. In hard weather or times of food shortage may occur in quite isolated and small clumps of conifers.

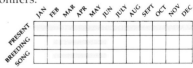

Habits and similar species: Able to remove cones and extract seeds with the crossed mandibles. Nests in January or February, so young hatch when cone-seeds plentiful. Most difficult time is summer when new crop of cones have yet to ripen. Scottish Crossbill confined to Scotland and has heavier bill; fond of Scot's Pine seeds. Parrot Crossbill slightly larger, has massive bill and deeper call.

Siskin
♂ ♀

SISKIN
Carduelis spinus L12cm
Characteristics: One of the smallest finches. Males have a bold black forehead and bib, yellow-green underside and rump, and yellow patches in the wings and tail. Females are less colourful and more streaked below, and like the juveniles, have no black on the head. Feeds silently, but utters a number of short, sweet sounding calls in flight and when moving through trees. Usual calls are 'tsuu' and a more excited twittering; the song is faster and longer, ending with a wheezing Greenfinch-like sound. Sometimes a short, fluttering, bat-like display-flight is performed.

Distribution and habitat: A fairly common breeding bird in northern Britain and Europe; prefers coniferous forests, especially tall spruce. A summer visitor to the far north and a winter visitor, sometimes in large numbers, to southern Britain and Europe.

	JAN	FEB	MAR	APR	MAY	JUN	JULY	AUG	SEPT	OCT	NOV	DEC
PRESENT												
BREEDING												
SONG												

Habits and similar species: Feeds on seeds, especially spruce and larch in summer, and on alder and birch in winter. Also visits bird tables and associates with other species, especially Redpoll. Nests high up in conifers, making a small cup of twigs, mosses and feathers. Serin is slightly smaller, and has yellow streaked back and flanks, but no black on head and does not show wing bars in flight.

111

♂ summer

Redpoll

♀ winter

REDPOLL
Carduelis flammea L13-15cm
Characteristics: A small finch with mostly brown streaked plumage and a characteristic red crown and black chin, a yellow bill and two pale wing bars. Males have a rosy breast and rump in the breeding season. Very variable in size and colourings with distinct races from different areas: birds from the northern race are paler and larger, birds from Greenland are largest and more heavily streaked and have a stouter bill. The calls are quiet and slightly metallic; song is composed of flight calls and a rapid trill.

Distribution and habitat: A common and widespread breeding bird of conifer plantations, birch and alder scrub, mixed open woodland. Summer visitor in north of range; winter visitor to southern Britain and most of Europe, frequenting alder woods.

	JAN	FEB	MAR	APR	MAY	JUN	JULY	AUG	SEPT	OCT	NOV	DEC
PRESENT												
BREEDING												
SONG												

Habits and similar species: Feeds on tree seeds, and rushes, docks and other prolific seed-producers. Forms large flocks in winter, sometimes of very large numbers when northern races flee harsh weather or poor seed crops. Nests in small trees, making neat cup of fine mosses and lichens. Arctic Redpoll rare vagrant from Greenland and far northern Scandinavia; white below, whiter wing bars, unstreaked rump.

OPEN COUNTRY

When the original woodland cover of lowland Europe was cleared for farming, vast areas of new habitats were created. The whole process took place over thousands of years, so some birds were able to adapt to the changes and survive in the hedgerows and much smaller areas of woodland which remained. Some bird species benefitted from the change, making use of the new open spaces which were created. The former slow pace of farming enabled them to breed in cultivated fields and to complete the development of their young before the harvest.

The pace of change of modern farming methods this century has been so great that many birds have been unable to adapt to the developments and are declining in numbers and contracting their ranges. The Corncrake is a damp meadow and grassland species, formerly widespread over Britain and Ireland, but it is now restricted to a few remote areas where the grassy meadows it breeds in are left uncut long enough for them to raise their young. Stone Curlews, which nest in more open, stony habitats, have also suffered from the tendency to cultivate fields much earlier in the season, and are restricted in Britain to a few areas of uncultivated land and special reserves. Gamebirds, like Partridges, nest below hedgerows at the edge of fields so they are less likely to be disturbed by early harvesting, but they have suffered from the use of pesticides which are a serious danger to newly-hatched young. Seed-eaters, which feed on fields after the harvest is taken, are now declining in certain areas where fields are cultivated immediately after harvesting, leaving little opportunity for finding left-over seeds. Buntings and sparrows are less common in areas of intensive farming as their winter food supply is very limited.

Mixed farming country with a patchwork of fields, hedgerows and coppices, and farm ponds and streams still provides good opportunities for a wide range of birds, and is a habitat which should be carefully managed.

The Fieldfare is a northern species which feeds on hedgerow berries in winter

113

CORNCRAKE
Crex crex L27cm

Characteristics: An extremely difficult bird to see, but its presence is betrayed by its unique call. A rasping 'crek crek', sounding more like a creaking machine than a bird, continues for hours on end during summer evenings, and more intermittently during the day. The volume increases and decreases as the bird turns its head from side to side and runs unseen through long grass. Often one bird answers another and then one of them may be glimpsed as it runs to meet a possible rival. In addition to the grating call there is also a cat-like squeal, sometimes given after a longer spell of 'crek crek' calls. If seen in flight the legs trail and the wings have a deep chestnut-red hue. The head and breast are grey and the flanks barred; females have more buff colouring below than males.

Distribution and habitat: A rare summer visitor to wet meadows in Ireland and west Scotland. Decreasing due to modern management techniques of early grass cutting, spraying and drainage.

Habits and similar species: Feeds on invertebrates and some plant material. Builds small nest of grasses; lays large clutch of 8-12 eggs, often destroyed by early rolling of fields. Water Rail similar size but longer bill, greyer underside and mostly confined to water.

Corn bunting

CORN BUNTING
Miliaria calandra L18cm

Characteristics: A solidly-built bird with a bulky bill. The plumage is uniformly greyish-brown and streaked, but lacks any noticeable features such as wing bars and rump-patches; in flight the wings do not show any pale trailing edge, and the tail is uniformly brown, unlike the larks and pipits. One noteworthy feature of the flying bird is the dangling legs which are quite conspicuous. The male's song is normally delivered from a prominent song perch such as a fence post or telegraph pole and has the air of someone jingling a bunch of keys. Calls include some harsh 'chip' and 'tsee' notes.

Distribution and habitat: A fairly common and widespread resident bird, fond of open grassy country and downland. More

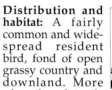

often found in dry rather than wet areas and is absent from uplands. Recent research has shown that it has an affinity with fields planted with barley.

	JAN	FEB	MAR	APR	MAY	JUN	JULY	AUG	SEPT	OCT	NOV	DEC
PRESENT												
BREEDING												
SONG												

Habits and similar species: Feeds mainly on small seeds, for which bill is specially adapted; has strong mandibles with a sharp S-shaped cutting edge. Will also take insects in summer when seeds are scarce. Nests on the ground, sometimes at base of a grass clump or bush, making a cup of woven grasses and hairs. Males often polygamous. Gathers in flocks in winter, sometimes with buntings and finches.

115

Yellowhammer

♀

♂

YELLOWHAMMER
Emberiza citrinella L16.5cm

Characteristics: The male has a splendid bright yellow head and underside; both male and female have a chestnut rump and very noticeable white outer tail feathers. Females have less intense yellow on the head and underside and a darker face. Juveniles are even less brightly coloured and are much more streaked than the male. In winter the male's colours are more subdued. The song is a characteristic 'A little bit of bread and no cheeeese' with the last note strongly accented and drawn out. Several short, rather quiet flight calls.

Distribution and habitat: A common and widespread breeding bird of farmland, hedgerows, open shrubby downland,

woodland edges and cliff tops. Resident over most of region, but a migrant in the far north, with birds moving south in large numbers in winter.

	JAN	FEB	MAR	APR	MAY	JUN	JULY	AUG	SEPT	OCT	NOV	DEC
PRESENT												
BREEDING												
SONG												

Habits and similar species: Feeds mainly on seeds, especially from cereal fields; also insects in summer or when feeding young. Nests in low bush, or sometimes on ground, making a cup of fine grasses and hairs. Corn Bunting lacks any yellow in its plumage and is larger. Reed Bunting also lacks yellow, has black head and white underside. Yellow-breasted Bunting has black face, brown nape, yellow underside.

Cirl bunting

♀ ♂

CIRL BUNTING
Emberiza cirlus L16.5cm
Characteristics: The male has a distinctive facial pattern with a black eyestripe and black throat, and differs from the male Yellowhammer by having a greyish-brown rump. The female and juvenile are both very similar to female Yellowhammer but also have a grey-brown, and not chestnut rump. The male's song is a rattling trill, mostly on a single note, and is often delivered from a high perch. Short 'tsip' calls are given by feeding birds.

Distribution and habitat: A very scarce breeding bird in the extreme south of England; more common in south-west Europe. In Britain mainly confined to coastal areas of mixed grassland and scrub; may join buntings feeding in large flocks on cereal fields in winter.

Habits and similar species: Feeds on seeds and small insects in summer. Nests in small bushes in scrub and makes a cup of mosses and leaves, lined with fine grasses. Rock Bunting has no yellow in plumage; face mainly white. Overlaps with Cirl Bunting in south-west Europe; very rare vagrant in Britain. Black-headed Bunting has all-black head and un-marked yellow breast; a very rare vagrant in Britain.

Red-legged partridge

imm.

RED-LEGGED PARTRIDGE
Alectoris rufa L34cm
Characteristics: A medium-sized gamebird with short rounded wings and a short rufous tail. The white bib framed with black and the strongly barred flanks are conspicuous when bird is on the ground, but red legs not always easy to see, usually being hidden in vegetation. At close range the black spotting on breast can be seen. Juveniles lack most of these features and look more like the Grey Partridge, but do not have yellowish horizontal streaks. Call is a rhythmic repetition of several hoarse notes, usually sounding like 'chuk chuker kuchuk cher'.

Distribution and habitat: Widespread on agricultural land and open stony grasslands, also rocky mountain slopes. In Britain it is an introduced species which has escaped as a game bird and is now well established in southern and central areas.

Habits and similar species: Feeds mainly on seeds and shoots; also takes insects, especially when young. Nests on ground in a hollow, usually partly concealed; lays a large clutch of 8-11 eggs. Chukar is very similar, but lacks the black spotting on the breast. This is also reared in game farms and escapes sometimes breed in the wild. The Rock Partridge is also very similar but has a whiter throat than the Chukar.

flight rear view

Partridge

♂ ♀ imm.

GREY PARTRIDGE
Perdix perdix L30cm
Characteristics: A medium-sized and compact gamebird with an unspotted grey breast, an orange face and flanks barred vertically with brown stripes and horizontally with faint yellow stripes. Males have a large brown horseshoe mark on the lower breast; females have a less distinct and smaller brown mark and in juveniles it is lacking completely. On spring evenings males make their loud grating 'kierrr-ik kierrr-ik' calls; if the bird is flushed it makes a rapid 'it-it-it' sound.

Distribution and habitat: A common and widespread breeding bird of a wide range of open habitats, especially mixed farmland with good hedgerows. Found in most of Britain and Europe apart from the far north and in very high uplands.

Habits and similar species: Feeds on seeds and shoots; will take insects. Builds nest on ground, usually concealing it in thick vegetation. Clutch may contain at least 10 eggs, sometimes as many as 20. Susceptible to pesticides and much reduced in some areas due to intensive farming methods. Juvenile Pheasants are plain brown; can be confused with juvenile Partridges, but long tail distinctive.

117

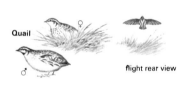

Quail ♀

♂ flight rear view

QUAIL
Coturnix coturnix L18cm
Characteristics: The smallest European gamebird and the only one to undertake regular migrations. A very difficult bird to see due to its diminutive size and secretive habits; it is also very difficult to flush, flying only at the last minute and then flies low over the ground, looking somewhat like a small brown wader with its surprisingly long wings. There is no red in the tail, as in Partridges. Males have a dark patch on the throat, females and juveniles have plain throats. Although difficult to see, the Quail can easily be detected by its distinctive piping call; it is often written as 'wet my lips'. This trisyllabic call can be heard throughout late spring and summer, but it is still difficult to pinpoint the bird.

Distribution and habitat: Once very widespread and common, it is now an unusual summer visitor, due to a loss of its favourite grassland habitats. May occur over much of Britain and Europe, but absent from the far north and most of Ireland.

Habits and similar species: Feeds mainly on seeds; also takes small invertebrates. Nests in a small hollow, using grass to line the nest, and lays a clutch of up to 12 eggs. Migrates across the Mediterranean to Africa. May be confused with chicks of other gamebirds, but is more likely, if seen, to be alone or in pairs, rather than in family groups. Juvenile Partridges are three times the size of adult Quail.

Montagu's harrier

imm.

♀

♂

MONTAGU'S HARRIER
Circus pygargus L41cm (male), 46cm (female)

Characteristics: A slim and elegant bird of prey with a graceful buoyant flight. The wings are long and pointed and the tail is long and parallel-sided. Males are noticeably smaller than females and have dark grey upperparts and breast, black wingtips, a single black bar on the upper wings and a double black bar below. Females are larger and have a barred brown tail and a crescent-shaped white rump. Immatures are also brown and streaked below on their rufous underparts. Not a very vocal bird, but does occasionally produce a shrill 'yik yik yik' call.

118

Distribution and habitat: A very scarce breeding bird in Britain, more widespread in Europe. Prefers open country, including farmland and heathland, with scattered trees and bushes. Sometimes in young conifer plantations. Migrates south to Africa in the autumn.

Habits and similar species: Catches a variety of small animals. Hunts low over the ground, quartering an area thoroughly, and dropping occasionally on to its prey. Nests on the ground in deep vegetation. Males are sometimes bigamous. Male Pallid Harrier is similar, but is paler and lacks dark wing bar; has smaller area of black on wing tips. Female Pallid is very similar to Montagu's but has dark throat ruff.

Cuckoo

CUCKOO
Cuculus canorus L33cm

Characteristics: Looks rather a like slim and pointed-winged raptor; in flight has a very straight back and tail, and wings always beat below the horizontal. Males mostly grey, but females have a more rusty tint and obvious barring across the upper breast. Some females are more strikingly rufous; can be distinguished from juveniles by absence of white nape patch. Male's 'cuckoo' call very familiar, females make an unusual bubbling sound.

Distribution and habitat: A common and familiar summer visitor to most of Britain and Europe, occurring in many habitats from reed-beds to moorlands. Woodlands, farm copses and hedgerows are also frequented. Usually avoids built-up areas.

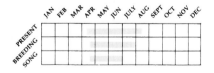

Habits and similar species: Feeds on large hairy caterpillars which are distasteful to most other birds, and takes many other insects. Makes no nest of its own, laying eggs singly in the nests of other birds. Females may lay up to 25 eggs in nests of much smaller birds such as Meadow Pipit, Dunnock, Reed Warbler and Spotted Flycatcher. Each female lays eggs in a particular host's nest and matches their egg colour.

pale subspecies

Barn owl

dark subspecies

Distribution and habitat: A once common bird of farmland and open country, but now scarce although still quite widespread. Numbers greatly reduced due to loss of rough grassland habitats, pesticides and lack of suitable breeding sites. Absent from the far north.

BARN OWL
Tyto alba L34cm
Characteristics: A very pale owl, white below and sandy-buff above with a white heart-shaped face and black eyes. There is a dark-breasted race which is darker and slightly flecked below. Flies buoyantly with legs dangling and tail and head slightly lower than the back. Makes a ghostly drawn-out screech, and various hissing and snoring sounds at the nest.

Habits and similar species: Feeds mainly on small mammals which it catches at night using its excellent hearing and sight. Will also hunt at dusk and dawn. Nests in old farm barns, church towers, hollow trees at edge of woods. No nest material is used, but eggs may be laid on a pile of discarded pellets.

119

Distribution and habitat: A very scarce breeding bird in Britain, but a common and widespread winter visitor. Breeds in open broad-leaved and coniferous woodland but in winter found in large flocks in more open country, especially agricultural land.

Fieldfare

juv.

FIELDFARE
Turdus pilaris L26cm
Characteristics: A large thrush with a grey head and rump, a dark reddish-brown back and a black tail. The underside is boldly spotted, but in flight the underwing is seen to be white. Mistle Thrush also has white underwing, but Fieldfare's flight call, a chuckling 'chak chak' is distinctive. Migrating flocks in spring may give their muted song; a very poor version of other thrush's songs.

Habits and similar species: An omnivore taking a great range of foods, from worms to berries. Feeds on the ground and in trees. Nests in trees, sometimes in loose colonies, using fine grasses and leaves and finishing with a mud lining. Migrates south in large flocks in late autumn, and often associates with other thrushes, Starlings and Golden Plover on farmland in winter.

STONE CURLEW
Burhinus oedicnemus L41cm

Characteristics: A mainly nocturnal bird with excellent camouflage; its mottled light brown plumage blends very well with the dry stony habitats it prefers, making it a very difficult bird to see. Its eyes are large and yellow and the deep yellow bill has a black tip. When alarmed it stands erect and these features are easily seen.The long legs are also yellow, but the most distinctive feature is a double white wing bar. From a distance the impression is of a stocky wader with a short neck and a large head. The call is heard at night and is reminiscent of the Curlew, but sounding more distant and melancholy. There are one or two variations on the curlew's 'curlee' and 'pee peerree'. There is also an excited and shrill alarm call, sounding like 'kee-weewee keeweewee keeweewee'.

Distribution and habitat: A scarce summer visitor to southern and eastern Britain, but commoner in southern and central Europe. Prefers dry stony heaths and sandy open areas, but also occurs on agricultural land.

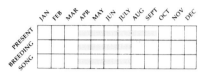

Habits and similar species: Feeds on worms, molluscs, insects and sometimes small mammals. Nests in the open on the ground in a small scrape, laying 2 eggs. No nesting material is used.

Redwing

juv.

REDWING
Turdus iliacus L20cm
Characteristics: Small thrush with distinctive facial markings; a cream-coloured eye-stripe and dark cheek patches separate it from other thrushes. The flanks and underwing are a rusty red colour and the underside is spotted. The upperparts are rather darker than the other thrushes. Song is rather like Song Thrush, but is in shorter snatches and can be even more repetitive. A thin 'tseep' flight note is often heard from migrating birds at night in autumn, and various short calls are made by feeding flocks.

Distribution and habitat: A scarce breeding bird in Scotland, but a common winter visitor to the rest of lowland Britain and Ireland as well as much of Europe. Breeds mainly in open upland birch forests in the far north including most of Scandinavia.

Habits and similar species: Takes a variety of foods, including many worms, insects and berries. Nests in a tree or bush, making a cup shaped nest lined with fine grasses. Forms mixed flocks with other thrushes in winter. Song Thrush is slightly larger and lacks eye stripe and red flanks. Very rare vagrant Eye-browed Thrush from Asia has reddish flanks and white eye-stripe, and is unspotted below.

Swallow

SWALLOW
Hirundo rustica L19cm
Characteristics: The deeply forked tail and chestnut throat and forehead are distinctive. The upperparts are a deep metallic blue and the underside is white. The tail is seen to have white spots in it at close range. Juveniles lack the long tail streamers but still show the white spots and the chestnut throat. Various short twittering calls are made in flight and there is usually a separate, more urgent-sounding call to warn of the approach of a predator.

Distribution and habitat: A common summer visitor to Britain and Europe, sometimes penetrating as far north as Iceland  and northern Norway. Found in many habitats, but especially farmland and the edges of villages and towns, where suitable nest sites can be found.

Habits and similar species: Catches insects on the wing, often very high up, but sometimes by swooping low. Colonial, gathering in very large flocks before migrating. Some gather in flocks of thousands. Saucer-like nest of mud and straw built under eaves and sometimes inside buildings on rafters. Red-rumped Swallow also has long tail streamers but red nape and red rump and no white spots in tail.

Lesser whitethroat

LESSER WHITETHROAT
Sylvia curruca L13.5cm
Characteristics: A greyer bird than the Whitethroat with a dark patch on the ear coverts contrasting with the grey head and white throat. The wings lack the rufous colouring of the Whitethroat and the underside looks paler. The song is similar to the Cirl Bunting's but is a less musical rattle, uttered from a concealed perch inside a bush. There is no song flight as in the Whitethroat and the bird is generally more secretive and difficult to observe, usually remaining in thick cover.

122

Distribution and habitat: A fairly common summer visitor to southern Britain and central Europe, preferring dense hedgerows and thick hawthorn scrub, sometimes young coniferous plantations. It may breed almost un-noticed in large shrubby gardens.

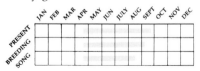

Habits and similar species: Feeds mainly on small invertebrates, but may take tiny berries in autumn. Nests deep inside a bush usually low down, building a cup-shaped nest out of small twigs and grass lined with hair. Migrates south in autumn when it may be easier to see in coastal scrub. Garden Warbler is more uniformly grey. Barred Warbler is larger and has greyer barred underside.

Garden warbler

GARDEN WARBLER
Sylvia borin L14cm
Characteristics: One of the least distinctive warblers, lacking any characteristics such as eye-stripes, wing-bars or rump patches. The head appears rather more rounded and the bill shorter than in other similar warblers. The colourings are mostly grey with a paler underside. The legs have a greyish-blue tinge. The song is a beautiful mellow warble, lower-pitched and often more prolonged than the very similar Blackcap's. A number of shorter and harsh-sounding contact and alarm notes are also given from dense cover.

Distribution and habitat: A common summer visitor to most of Britain and Europe apart from the extreme north and west. Breeds in woodland edges and clearings, thick hedgerows and shrubby gardens. The nest is built at the base of a dense bush and is a cup of grasses lined with hairs.

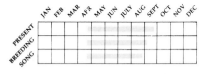

Habits and similar species: Feeds on insects and in autumn takes small fruits and berries prior to migration. Spends most of its time in dense cover. Blackcap is very similar but has black or brown cap. Leaf warblers like Willow Warbler and Chiffchaff occur in same habitats but songs are distinctive and they are slimmer with greener plumage.

Blackcap ♂

♀

BLACKCAP
Sylvia atricapilla L14cm

Characteristics: Most recognisable feature is the male's black cap. Immature males have a blackish-brown cap and females and juveniles have a brown cap. In all cases the cap colouring does not extend below eye level. The upperparts are a plain greyish-brown with no distinguishing marks and the underside is paler. Several sharp 'chack' alarm and scold notes are made and the song is a beautifully melodious warble, given in short snatches.

Distribution and habitat: A common summer visitor to most of Britain and Europe apart from the far north. Most individuals migrate south for the winter, but a small number stay in southern Britain. Prefers woodland edges, hedgerows, mature gardens and scrub.

	JAN	FEB	MAR	APR	MAY	JUN	JULY	AUG	SEPT	OCT	NOV	DEC
PRESENT												
BREEDING												
SONG												

Habits and similar species: Feeds on insects, and in autumn and winter takes small fruits and berries. May be more frequent in gardens in winter. Nests in low vegetation building a cup of leaves and grasses. Garden Warbler is very similar apart from lacking black or brown cap. Marsh and Willow Tits have black caps but they have white faces and shorter bills.

123

Dartford warbler

♂

DARTFORD WARBLER
Sylvia undata L12.5cm

Characteristics: First impressions are of a small dark bird with a long tail. Its skulking habits make this a difficult warbler to watch, but in spring males sit on a prominent perch to sing, and then the purple-brown underside, red eye, white-spotted throat and white-edged tail are more clearly seen. Females are more retiring and are generally paler and browner than the males. The song is delivered from a perch on top of a bush or sometimes from a short song flight and is an excited churring chatter.

Distribution and habitat: A scarce breeding bird in Britain, confined to the far south, commoner in south west Europe and Italy. In Britain, occurs in dry open heaths, with stands of mature heather and gorse, also a variety of dry open country in Europe.

	JAN	FEB	MAR	APR	MAY	JUN	JULY	AUG	SEPT	OCT	NOV	DEC
PRESENT												
BREEDING												
SONG												

Habits and similar species: Feeds on insects, spiders, small invertebrates. Nests in thick bushes such as gorse, usually low down. Very susceptible to harsh winters and habitat destruction, and British population is at northern limit of its range. Marmora's Warbler is very similar, but lacks purple-brown underside and white undertail feathers. A very rare vagrant to Britain, confined to Mediterranean coast.

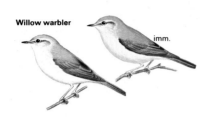

Willow warbler

imm.

WILLOW WARBLER
Phylloscopus trochilus L11cm
Characteristics: Common warbler and easily detected by its characteristic song which it sings as soon as it arrives on its breeding grounds in spring. The brown-grey upperparts are tinged with green and the underside has a yellowish hue, especially in juveniles. There are no wing bars and only a pale supercilium. The legs are a flesh colour, but may sometimes be tinged with darker brown. A constant 'hoo-eet' call note is given from within dense cover and the song is given from a more prominent perch. Song starts with a few high notes and then continues on a descending scale and gradually fades away with a quieter flourish.

Distribution and habitat: A widespread breeding bird over most of Britain and northern Europe, occurring in a range of

habitats wherever there are just a few trees and lower bushes such as woodland edges and clearings, hedgerows, mature gardens and parks.

Habits and similar species: An active bird searching for insects in shrubby vegetation, sometimes making short flycatcher-like dashes after insects. Nests on ground below thick vegetation making domed, grassy structure. Very secretive near the nest but will mob intruders. Chiffchaff is very similar but call and leg colour are different. Wood Warbler also has different call and is greener above, whiter below.

124

Chiffchaff

CHIFFCHAFF
Phylloscopus collybita L11cm
Characteristics: Common warbler and almost identical in appearance to the Willow Warbler, best distinguished by its call; an incessantly repeated 'chiff chaff' or 'tsip tsap'. Occasional variations are 'chiff chiff chaff'. The 'huEET' call note is very similar to the Willow Warbler's but less markedly di-syllabic, emphasizing the second syllable slightly more. The legs are dark, compared with the Willow Warbler's flesh-coloured legs, and the plumage has less green and yellow in it. The impression of a bird seen in good light is of a duller, slightly worn version of the Willow Warbler. Northern birds, sometimes seen on autumn migration in the south have a much greyer appearance.

Distribution and habitat: A very common summer visitor to Britain and Europe except the far north. A few overwinter in

southern Britain and south-west Europe. Occurs in a wide range of shrubby habitats, especially hedgerows, woodland edges and large gardens.

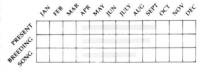

Habits and similar species: A lively bird, searching for insects in low vegetation and sometimes higher up in the canopy. In winter often near water. Nests just above ground level in a dense bush making a domed construction of grasses and leaves. Leg colour and song tell it from Willow Warbler. Greenish Warbler, a vagrant to Britain, very similar but has pale wing bar and slightly more conspicuous eye-stripe.

Skylark

SKYLARK
Alauda arvensis L18cm

Characteristics: A large lark with a hint of a crest, not always visible in the field. Mostly brown and mottled above, with a buff-coloured streaked breast and white underside. The tail is edged with white and in flight looks dark below. Juveniles have shorter tail and no crest. The most striking feature is the song, delivered from a high and soaring song flight, and given whilst ascending, hovering and descending. It can be heard from first light until late evening and often in chorus as many birds take to the air at once.

Distribution and habitat: A common and widespread bird over most of Britain and Europe, resident everywhere except for northern Europe and Scandinavia. A mass migration westwards occurs in autumn. Found in open agricultural land, grasslands and coastal marshes.

Habits and similar species: Feeds on small invertebrates and seeds collected on the ground. May congregate in large flocks, especially in fields after harvest in autumn and winter. Nests on the ground, sometimes beside a tussock of grass, making a cup of grasses. Woodlark is similar, but has no white outer tail feathers. Crested Lark has much more prominent crest and sings from the ground or a rock.

Little owl

LITTLE OWL
Athene noctua L23cm

Characteristics: A small compact owl with noticeably spotted upperparts and a paler spotted underside. The eyes are large and yellow and there are no ear tufts. The darker facial disc gives a fierce expression. In flight the wings appear rounded and the tail short; the flight pattern is undulating with bouts of wingbeats interspersed with short glides with closed wings. Strange mewing calls are given throughout the day and at night, with the bird often perched on a prominent post.

Distribution and habitat: A fairly common breeding bird over southern Britain and most of Europe. Successfully colonised Britain after introduction in 1880s. Common in parkland, farmland with hedgerows, open woodland and rocky areas like scrub-covered sea-cliffs.

Habits and similar species: Perches in the open on poles, low bushes, wires and drops on to prey such as beetles, earthworms, some small mammals and birds. May sometimes hover to catch moths at dusk. Nests in a hole in a tree or stony bank. Scops Owl is slightly smaller and has short ear tufts, more uniform colouring and unspotted upperparts; call is an incessantly repeated monotonous whistle.

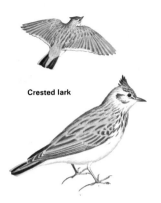

Crested lark

CRESTED LARK
Galerida cristata L17cm
Characteristics: Recognised by its conspicuous crest which is long and always erect. Juveniles also have a crest but the tail is shorter than in the adult. The tail has buff, not white, outer feathers. In flight the orange-buff patch on the underwing contrasts with the white underside. The call is a fluty trisyllabic 'whee-whee-ooo' and the song is much shorter and more melancholy than the Skylark's, usually delivered from a low perch.

Distribution and habitat: Prefers dry open land, often cultivated, roadsides, often found near towns. Only a rare vagrant to Britain, but widespread and fairly common throughout much of Europe, as far north as southern Scandinavia.

Habits and similar species: Catches insects on the ground and also feeds on tiny seeds. Nests on the ground, usually near a small clump of grass or prominent stone, building a cup-shaped nest. Thekla Lark is similar and difficult to distinguish in the field, but has Skylark-like song delivered from fluttering flight or high perch. Confined to extreme south-west Europe and avoids towns and habitations.

126

Magpie

MAGPIE
Pica pica L46cm
Characteristics: Black-and-white pattern and very long tail, making up half the length of the body, are easily spotted characteristics; no other land bird has this combination. In good light and at close range the tail is seen to have a greenish gloss and the body feathers have a purple-blue gloss. Flight is uneven with rapid fluttering wing beats; on the ground movement is lively with much hopping and side-stepping. Chattering calls are frequently given, and also imitated by Jays.

Distribution and habitat: Very common and widespread over most of Britain, except the extreme north, and most of Europe. Occurs in woodland margins, agricultural land with hedgerows and trees, and increasingly in towns and cities.

Habits and similar species: Takes a wide variety of foods and is an opportunist feeder. Fruits, seeds, insects, carrion and small birds are all taken in season. Some birds are learning to scavenge in towns, but usually avoid human contact. Builds a large domed nest of twigs deep in a large bush. Azure-winged Magpie has black head, long blue tail, blue wings and buff body; confined to south-west Europe.

imm.
Rook

ROOK
Corvus frugilegus L46cm

Characteristics: A large all black bird with a bare whitish face patch. In good light the plumage shows a deep purple gloss unlike the blacker Carrion Crow. The feathers on the thighs are fluffed out to give the appearance of baggy trousers. In profile the bill is seen to be finer and more dagger-like than the Crow's. There is no song, but Rooks produce a number of harsh 'caah' and 'caaw' sounds, plus a number of other less-frequently heard harsh notes.

Distribution and habitat: Common and widespread on agricultural land over most of Britain and Europe, but absent from far northern Britain and most of Scandinavia, and only a summer visitor to northern Europe. May be some movement west in very harsh winters.

Habits and similar species: A highly gregarious bird, nesting and feeding in large groups. Takes a wide range of soil invertebrates and seeds from agricultural land. Nests in large colonies in tops of tall trees, and sometimes in pylons, usually near the edges of woods or in isolated clumps of trees. A few birds sometimes nest away from the main colony. The nest is a large cup of twigs lined with grass and leaves.

CARRION CROW
Corvus corone L47cm

Characteristics: Large all black bird with a heavy black beak. Unlike the Rook, there is no purple gloss to the plumage, although the feathers are very shiny, sometimes there is a hint of deep blue. The thigh feathers are sleek with no 'leggings' effect and the face is all black without any bare patches. The most frequently heard call is a harsh 'kraaa', often repeated 3 times. Several other harsh notes are also produced. On the ground Crows make clumsy hopping and walking movements; flight is heavy and direct. Tail is square-ended while the Raven in flight has a wedge-shaped tail.

Distribution and habitat: A common resident in most of Britain and western Europe, but replaced in Ireland, the north and the rest of Europe by the Hooded Crow, which is a race of the same species. Found in most types of country, apart from high altitudes and deserts.

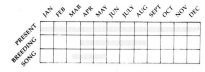

Habits and similar species: Feeds on a great range of foods and is an opportunist, taking carrion, fruits and seeds, invertebrates, small birds and mammals. Much persecuted. Nests in a tall tree, sometimes on a cliff, never in a colony. Normally solitary or in pairs, forms small family groups late in summer. Raven is much larger with more solid-looking bill. Jackdaw is smaller with shorter bill and grey nape.

MOUNTAINS, MOORLANDS AND HEATHS

In winter, upland regions can be very inhospitable and few birds will be found there. Some, like the Ptarmigan, moult into white winter plumage to cope with the snow and have special adaptations for withstanding the cold, such as feathered feet, but many other birds leave high ground and seek shelter and food in the lowlands until the spring.

In spring, a variety of bird species, as varied as waders, thrushes and finches, migrate to the uplands to breed. Most will nest on the ground or in crevices, making use of whatever cover is available. The lack of disturbance is one of the most important reasons for breeding in uplands, and many species find little of their usual food whilst they are there; they may have to change their feeding habits completely if, like the Curlew, they are more suited to feeding on mudflats on the coast. Sheer cliffs and mountain ledges provide safe nest sites for birds of prey, like eagles, which can range over vast distances searching for food. Many of their nest sites are ancestral, having been occupied continuously for a great many years.

129

Moorlands managed for grouse are good breeding areas for other species, especially ground-nesting birds of prey like the Merlin and Hen Harrier; sadly, they still suffer persecution from gamekeepers and are not always successful. Pipits and larks also benefit from the maintenance of heather moorland, and Wheatears and Whinchats join them in summer to feed on the abundant insect life.

Lowland heath is a drier, warmer habitat than moorland and provides unique conditions where insects can thrive,attracting specialist insectivorous birds like the Nightjar and other insect and seed eaters which nest on the ground or in low vegetation. Heathland is a rapidly diminishing habitat and the areas which remain are in urgent need of conservation as several heathland birds are unable to survive in other habitats.

The Golden Plover is a typical upland breeding bird which winters in large flocks on lowland farms.

Golden eagle

imm.

GOLDEN EAGLE
Aquila chrysaetos L75-88cm
Characteristics: A very large bird of prey with mostly brown plumage but a paler head. In flight wings look very long and have splayed out tips, and when gliding and soaring are held in a very shallow 'V'. Powerful flight with 6 or 7 wing beats followed by a short glide. May stay airborne for hours on end. Juveniles have more white in wings and tail than adult.

Distribution and habitat: Found in mountainous regions in Scotland and most of Europe. Never common. Frequently persecuted and declining in much of its range. Nests on cliffs or tops of large trees, often using ancestral site adding yearly to large pile of twigs.

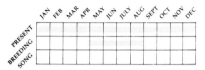

Habits and similar species: Soars and glides over open mountainous country in search of food, taking medium-sized birds and mammals such as grouse and rabbits, but also takes carrion and occasionally young deer. White-tailed Eagle has shorter white tail and broader wings.

ROUGH-LEGGED BUZZARD
Buteo lagopus L51-61cm
Characteristics: Similar to Buzzard, but has tail with one terminal dark band and no barring, paler underwing with conspicuous black carpal patches and a paler head and neck. Dark breast band may also be distinctive, but some Buzzards show this feature also. Legs are feathered. More inclined to hover than Buzzard and has louder call. Sometimes gives impression of harrier.

Distribution and habitat: Breeds on tundra in northern Scandinavia and Europe, moving south and west for the winter and then preferring open flat country. Population increases in good vole years. Nests in a tree or a ledge in open areas building large platform of twigs.

Habits and similar species: Feeds mostly on small mammals like voles and lemmings which it is able to find whilst hovering briefly. Moves as far west as the east coast of Britain in winter when it mostly occurs on coastal marshes. Long-legged Buzzard is a North African species also found in the eastern Mediterranean and occasionally elsewhere; sometimes quite rufous, has an unbarred tail and is larger.

Hen harrier
upper views

♀   ♂

HEN HARRIER
Circus cyaneus L43-51cm
Characteristics: The male has plain pale grey plumage with black wing-tips and small white rump patch. Females and immatures are brown with a white rump and barred tail. Adult females larger than males and have slightly owl-like face. A chattering 'kek-kek-kek' alarm call is also sometimes given as a display. The flight is light and relaxed; the wings look more rounded than in other harriers, and females flying high can look very similar to Sparrowhawk.

Distribution and habitat: A scarce breeding bird in northern Britain and Europe and a summer visitor to Scandinavia. Migrates south and west in winter. Breeds on open moorland and young conifer plantations. In winter may move to lower altitudes.

	JAN	FEB	MAR	APR	MAY	JUN	JULY	AUG	SEPT	OCT	NOV	DEC
PRESENT												
BREEDING												
SONG												

Habits and similar species: Feeds on small birds and mammals caught on the ground, but sometimes pursues small birds when they are flushed. Nests on the ground in low vegetation, males sometimes polygamous. Montagu's Harrier is slightly smaller and slimmer and males have dark wing bar. Female Montagu's very similar, but also slimmer with narrower more pointed wings and less white on rump.

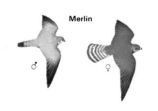

Merlin

♂   ♀

MERLIN
Falco columbarius L27-33cm
Characteristics: The smallest European bird of prey with the least distinctive markings. The male has a streaked underside and plainer grey upperparts and a dark terminal band on the tail. The larger female is dark brown above and paler below with a streaked underside and barred tail. The flight is fast and dashing especially when in pursuit of small birds; it hovers occasionally and also soars very high up when it has a similar outline to Peregrine. Makes a shrill repetitive alarm call similar to Kestrel.

Distribution and habitat: A scarce resident and summer visitor to Britain with some birds passing through on passage in autumn. Breeds in open country, especially moorland, young conifer plantations, and may move to lower altitudes and the coast in winter.

	JAN	FEB	MAR	APR	JUN	JULY	AUG	SEPT	OCT	NOV	DEC
PRESENT												
BREEDING												
SONG												

Habits and similar species: An agile bird in the air, able to pursue and catch small birds like pipits, but may take other prey. Nests on the ground, but sometimes in an old crow's nest. A declining species due to pesticide poisoning, habitat loss and persecution. Hobby is larger and longer winged and more likely to be seen chasing insects. Bold facial markings and heavily streaked underside show well in flight.

Snowy owl

SNOWY OWL
Nyctea scandiaca L53-66cm
Characteristics: Huge white owl, unmistakable when seen, but despite its large size is rather shy and may be overlooked when it sits motionless on ground. Females are noticeably larger than males and are barred with black dots, although they are still mostly white. Juveniles are more densely spotted, may look grey at a distance, especially when seen against a snowy background. Male produces a harsh barking call and a deep hoot, and females produce a higher-pitched bark.

Distribution and habitat: Breeds on tundra and moorland in the Arctic, but has bred as far south as Shetland. Moves away from high arctic breeding grounds in winter, and irruptions occur when lemming populations fail. The nest is a scrape in the ground.

Habits and similar species: Hunts small mammals and birds, taking lemmings and voles and also adult and young waders and Ptarmigan. Often seen during the day, but is very active just after dusk. The Great Grey Owl is similar in size but has much darker mainly grey plumage and prominent facial disc.

Short-eared owl

SHORT-EARED OWL
Asio flammeus L38cm
Characteristics: A long-winged mostly brown owl often seen in flight over open country during the day. Despite its name the ear-tufts are not easy to see in the field, but the pale yellow eyes are sometimes more obvious. The wings show dark patches at the elbow both above and below. The flight is harrier-like and involves soaring and gliding and a wing-clapping display. Its harsh barking call is sometimes heard in flight. The deep 'hoo hoo hoo' call is also given in flight, mostly whilst in display over a territory.

Distribution and habitat: A widespread resident over much of Britain and Europe. A summer visitor to the far north, and a winter visitor to southern Britain and southern Europe. Occurs on moorland, young conifer plantations and in winter on coastal marshes.

Habits and similar species: Very active by day, seen quartering low over moorland and rough grassland in search of small mammals and sometimes birds. Nests on the ground in a scrape. In winter may congregate in small groups on good feeding grounds and when not hunting may then be seen sitting on the ground in the open. Tawny Owl is shorter winged and plumper and much more nocturnal.

DOTTEREL
Charadrius morinellus L23cm
Characteristics: A medium-sized wader with white eye-stripes meeting in a 'V' on the back of the neck. The underside is mostly chestnut darkening to black on the lower belly and the legs are yellow. Females are slightly larger than males and more brightly coloured; they do the courting and the more subdued males do the incubation and take care of the young. Juveniles lack the chestnut and black breast markings, but they do have the white eye-stripes and breast band. A quiet 'wit-e-wee' call is repeated many times by females in flight.

Distribution and habitat: A scarce breeding bird of high mountains in Scotland, but is commoner in Scandinavia; also in some scattered sites in the Alps. More likely to be seen as a passage migrant in southern parts of Britain; overwinters in north Africa.

Habits and similar species: The male is extremely confiding on the nest, females are more likely to run or fly when approached. Nests on the ground on tundra, high bare mountain plateaus, usually not close to water. Feeds on small invertebrates. Often visits traditional sites on passage before completing migration to breeding grounds. Golden Plover is larger and has black chest and belly.

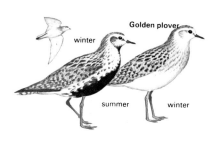

GOLDEN PLOVER
Pluvialis apricaria L27cm
Characteristics: A plump wader with a prominent black face and breast bordered with white; outside the breeding season the underside is much paler and streaked. Northern breeding birds have much more white bordering the black than southern birds. The back is speckled yellow-brown and the underwing is white. The mournful song is given during a display flight; a rhythmic 'plu-eee-u, plu-eee-u' is sometimes followed by 'per-poo-ria' with the second syllable accented.

Distribution and habitat: A fairly common breeding bird in upland areas in Britain, Iceland and Scandinavia. In winter moves to lower altitudes and often feeds on agricultural land in mixed flocks with Lapwings. Nests on the ground in a shallow scrape.

Habits and similar species: Takes many soil invertebrates, especially earthworms. Widely dispersed over breeding grounds but forms large flocks in winter, often associating with other birds. Migrating flocks fly in a loose 'V' formation. American Golden Plover is a vagrant from North America with grey underwing. Pacific Golden Plover from Asia and Alaska is smaller, slimmer and has longer legs.

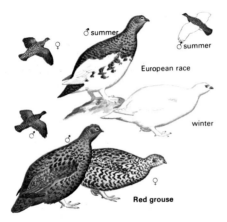

Distribution and habitat: A common resident on heather moorland at high altitude in the south, but nearer sea level in the north. In Britain moorlands are managed to provide ample young heather for the grouse. Nests on the ground in a scrape using grasses.

RED GROUSE
Lagopus lagopus scoticus L38-41cm
Characteristics: A gamebird with rich brown plumage and feathered legs. Females have less red in the plumage and males have bright red wattles in summer. The wings look darker than the body in flight. The voice is a harsh staccato 'go-back, go-back' often given as a bird skims away. This grouse is a race of European Willow Grouse, *L. l. lagopus*, which is white in winter and has white wings and belly in summer.

	JAN	FEB	MAR	APR	MAY	JUN	JULY	AUG	SEPT	OCT	NOV	DEC
PRESENT												
BREEDING												
SONG												

Habits and similar species: Feeds mainly on heather shoots but will sometimes take other vegetation. Young are taken away from the nest soon after hatching. Ptarmigan lives at higher altitude and is greyer in summer with dark tail. Black Grouse is larger and males are mostly black, females brown with darker barring.

134

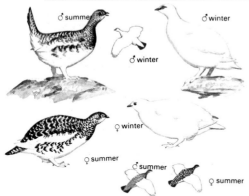

Distribution and habitat: Confined to open stony mountain slopes where the vegetation is sparse and consists mainly of lichens. In winter may descend to lower altitudes. At high altitude in Scotland and the Alps, but lower down in Iceland and Scandinavia.

PTARMIGAN
Lagopus mutus L35cm
Characteristics: All white in winter with heavily feathered legs and feet. Tail is black and males have black patch through eye and red wattle. Summer plumage is greyer above with darker mottlings in male and more rufous colouring in female, wings and underside are still mostly white. In autumn both male and female turn greyer on upperparts. The call consists mainly of grating 'arrr arrr' sounds.

	JAN	FEB	MAR	APR	MAY	JUN	JULY	AUG	SEPT	OCT	NOV	DEC
PRESENT												
BREEDING												
SONG												

Habits and similar species: Feeds on leaves and shoots and in autumn takes berries. Scrapes snow away to find buds in winter. Rarely descends as low as tree line but may leave high mountain tops in harsh winters. Nests on the ground in a shallow scrape using very little nest material. Winter Willow Grouse is very similar but has stouter bill, less feathering on toes and no black patch between bill and eye.

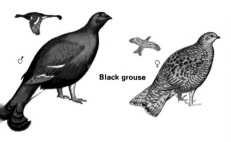

Black grouse

BLACK GROUSE
Tetrao tetrix L53cm (male) 41cm (female)

Characteristics: The male is a large black gamebird with a curious lyre-shaped tail, a white wing bar and white patches on the shoulder and under the tail. The female, known as the Greyhen is smaller with a forked tail, and a narrow and rather indistinct wing bar. Males produce a di-syllabic sneezing call and females make an almost pheasant-like 'kok kok' sound. Males display at a lek, sometimes in large numbers, and perform a dance in which the tail is fanned out. Females come to the lek for mating and then disperse to safe nesting sites.

Distribution and habitat: A fairly common resident bird in upland forest clearings, moorland and open birch and pine woods. Absent from Ireland and south west Europe and becoming scarce in some parts of Britain. Nests on the ground in a shallow scrape.

	JAN	FEB	MAR	APR	MAY	JUN	JULY	AUG	SEPT	OCT	NOV	DEC
PRESENT												
BREEDING												
SONG												

Habits and similar species: Feeds on buds and shoots and takes fruits and berries in season. Especially fond of birch buds. Females alone take care of the young. Capercaillie is much larger; male is greyer and lacks lyre-shaped tail, female has richer rufous brown plumage with chestnut breast patch.

Wheatear

WHEATEAR
Oenanthe oenanthe L14.5cm

Characteristics: Small land-bird with a striking black and white tail pattern. In flight dark wings and characteristic tail pattern give the impression of a black and white bird. In summer the male has a grey back and black cheeks with a white eye-stripe. The female also has the eye stripe, but has browner upperparts and warm buff colourings below. The song is a rather scratchy warble sometimes given from a stone and sometimes from a short song flight. It may often be heard at night. The Greenland race is slightly larger with a heavier bill and richer colours.

Distribution and habitat: A common summer visitor often arriving early in spring and still present in late autumn. Breeds in a variety of rocky habitats from sea cliffs and islands to open upland areas. Prefers areas with open turf to feed in. Nests in rock crevice or rabbit burrow.

	JAN	FEB	MAR	APR	MAY	JUN	JULY	AUG	SEPT	OCT	NOV	DEC
PRESENT												
BREEDING												
SONG												

Habits and similar species: Feeds on insects and invertebrates mostly collected from the ground but will make short dashes into the air after more active insects. Male may stand guard near incubating female. Black-eared Wheatear is vagrant from Mediterranean and has creamy-buff plumage, black cheeks and wings and black centre to tail. Some males can be almost white in breeding season.

BLUETHROAT
Luscinia svecica L14cm

Characteristics: A nervous robin-sized bird with rusty-red patches at the base of the tail and a prominent supercilium. The male's blue throat has a bright lustre and depending on the race has either a white or a red spot in the centre. In the winter the male's blue throat lacks the spot and is duller. Females have a cream throat with a darker border. Juveniles lack the blue throat but still show the rust-red patches at the base of the tail.

Distribution and habitat: A scarce passage migrant in Britain, with mostly juveniles or winter adults passing through. Breeds on tundra and in swampy thickets near freshwater, and also in sub-alpine birch forest. Nests on the ground beneath vegetation.

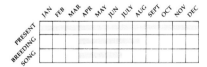

Habits and similar species: Feeds on insects and small seeds, usually collected from the ground. Migrates south in autumn and may turn up on coasts. Impossible to separate different races when male's throat colour fades. Female Black Redstart which has whole of tail and rump rust-red and female Redstart with paler colours but also with red tail and rump; neither have white eye-stripes or throat markings.

Twite

♂ summer

♀ winter

TWITE
Carduelis flavirostris L13.5cm

Characteristics: A small finch with mostly brown plumage, black legs and a whitish wing bar. The male has a buff throat and a pink rump, although this is a difficult feature to see in the field. In autumn it becomes even less distinct. In winter the bill is yellow but is greyer in summer. The voice is similar to the Linnet's but there is also a nasal 'twa-it' call which gives the bird its name and is often heard when birds are in flocks. The song is a quiet chattering medley which also includes the call.

Distribution and habitat: A fairly common breeding bird on uplands and also in coastal areas in the far north. Confined mainly to northern Britain and Scandinavia, but in winter disperses to lower altitudes and coastal areas. A separate race occurs in Turkey.

Habits and similar species: Feeds on small seeds collected from the ground and by perching in low vegetation. In winter may congregate in mixed flocks on waste ground. Often flies off for some distance when disturbed and can be difficult to observe for any length of time. Nests in a low bush. Sometimes in loose colonies. Linnet similar but is more confined to lowlands; male has grey head, and red crown.

Ring ouzel

♀

♂

RING OUSEL
Turdus torquatus L24cm
Characteristics: Similar to Blackbird but with large crescent-shaped white throat patch and pale wing panel. On closer examination is not so uniformly black as male Blackbird. Some partially albino male Blackbirds may have white crescent, but the black areas will be blacker than in the Ring Ousel. Female is browner than male and has slightly mottled white crescent. Juveniles have white throat and spotted breast. Makes harsh 'chack chack' call, and song is a simple, sad-sounding 'tee-lyu tee-lyu tee-lyu'.

Distribution and habitat: A fairly common summer visitor to rocky upland areas and alpine spruce forests. Usually found where there is some low vegetation and berry-bearing shrubs. Nests on or near the ground in thick vegetation or under rock overhangs.

Habits and similar species: Feeds on invertebrates and berries. Hops on the ground in search of food but also feeds in rowan and other berry-bearing trees in autumn. Normally very wary and will not allow close approach; forms small flocks in autumn and mixes with other thrushes on migration when it may be seen on coasts.

Hooded crow

HOODED CROW
Corvus corone cornix L46cm
Characteristics: The same species as the Carrion Crow but a different race, occurring mainly in areas where the Carrion Crow is not present. Where the two races do occur together inter-breeding takes place and hybrids arise. The Hooded Crow has a grey body and black head and wings, but hybrids may look darker with some spotting on the grey areas. Its flight is fairly re-laxed with steady shallow wingbeats. It is usually seen singly or in pairs, but larger groups sometimes gather near good sources of food. The voice is the same as the Carrion Crow with several harsh notes.

Distribution and habitat: Confined in Britain to north-west Scotland, Ireland and the Isle of Man, but much more widespread in the eastern half of Europe. Found in agricultural areas as well as uplands where sheep are farmed. Nests in trees, making a large cup of twigs.

Habits and similar species: An omni-vorous species taking a great range of foods, especially carrion and refuse, and also raiding nests in summer. Much persecuted and very wary of man. Birds from the far north of Europe migrate south and west in winter, sometimes turning up on the east coast of England. Jackdaw is much smaller and has a grey nape, but rest of body is dark.

Hobby

imm.

HOBBY
Falco subbuteo L30-36cm
Characteristics: Small bird of prey with a flight silhouette similar to a swift with long scythe-like wings and a relatively short tail. The underparts are boldly streaked and the thighs and undertail coverts are rufous, especially in the male. The male's upperparts are dark slaty-grey, female and juveniles are browner. The white throat and cheeks contrast with the bold moustachial stripes. The flight is swift and agile, enabling the Hobby to catch swallows and martins. It sometimes flies low when the wings are beaten very powerfully. The call is a shrill and frantic 'chi-chi-chi-chi..........'

138

Distribution and habitat: A summer visitor to southern Britain and most of Europe apart from the far north and high altitudes.

Usually found on open country, including heathland, near woodland. Nests in an old crow's nest, using no material of its own.

Habits and similar species: Hunts small birds in the air, and often catches dragonflies on the wing, eating them whilst still in flight. May circle or soar, but never hovers. A long-distance migrant, arriving in May and leaving in September. Red-footed Falcon is similar but male has dark unstreaked breast, darker upperparts and chestnut thighs and undertail coverts. Female Red-foot has rufous crown.

northern race

southern race

Great grey shrike

GREAT GREY SHRIKE
Lanius excubitor L24cm
Characteristics: The largest shrike with black, white and grey plumage. Can be variable with several different races. There may be a white stripe above the eye and one or two white wing bars. The tail is graduated and is black with a white border. The bill is slightly hooked. The harsh 'chack chack' alarm call is given when predators appear, and there is also a fairly restrained song containing some mimicry.

Distribution and habitat: A scarce winter visitor to Britain usually found in open areas with scattered bushes. Resi-

dent in much of Europe and a summer visitor to the far north. Breeds in rough open country, nesting in thorny bushes.

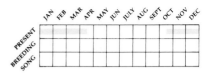

Habits and similar species: Catches large insects, lizards, voles, etc, and often impales them on thorns in a 'larder' which may contain several prey items. Makes itself very obvious by sitting on the highest point of a prominent bush and looks very white from a distance. Lesser Grey Shrike is smaller and has all black forehead; posture is usually more upright. A scarce visitor to Britain from southern Europe.

Woodchat shrike

imm.

WOODCHAT SHRIKE
Lanius senator L17cm
Characteristics: The rich chestnut crown and nape distinguish this from the other shrikes. Both male and female have a striking black and white wing pattern, although the colours are brighter in the male. Juveniles look more like the juveniles of other shrikes but have a more scaly appearance and show a pale wing patch. A sharp 'chip' call is given when alarmed and there is a quite musical, rather scratchy, song containing plenty of mimicry, with each phrase repeated up to 5 times.

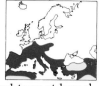

Distribution and habitat: A scarce vagrant in Britain usually appearing in early summer at coastal sites. Breeds in dry open country with scattered trees at low altitudes; a summer visitor to southern Europe. Nests in the outer branches of a tree making a cup of twigs.

	JAN	FEB	MAR	APR	MAY	JUN	JULY	AUG	SEPT	OCT	NOV	DEC
PRESENT												
BREEDING												
SONG												

Habits and similar species: Sits in a prominent position, sometimes on wires and high posts, searching for insects, lizards and small birds. May use barbed wire to spear prey. Masked Shrike has black crown and white forehead, white wing patches and outer tail, and orange-brown flanks.

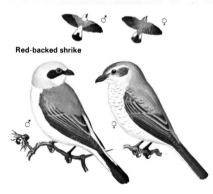

Red-backed shrike

RED-BACKED SHRIKE
Lanius collurio L18cm
Characteristics: Only European shrike with a chestnut back. Both sexes share this feature but males have a grey head and black mask, females and juveniles have browner heads. The male's underside is white with a warm buff-red tone and the female and juvenile have buff underparts with a scalloped appearance. The male's black tail has white edges near the base; female's tail is browner. The alarm call is a harsh 'chack' and the song is a quiet warble.

Distribution and habitat: A very scarce bird in Britain, probably extinct in the south but may be colonising east Scotland. More widespread in Europe and fairly common in dry open country with scattered bushes and trees. Nests deep inside a prickly bush.

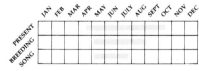

	JAN	FEB	MAR	APR	MAY	JUN	JULY	AUG	SEPT	OCT	NOV	DEC
PRESENT												
BREEDING												
SONG												

Habits and similar species: Sits on a prominent bush looking for prey which may be large insects, lizards, frogs, nestling birds. Surplus prey stored on spines of a thorny bush. Juvenile Woodchat and Red-backed Shrikes are very similar, but Woodchat has pale wing bar, and Red-backed has less scaly appearance.

Meadow pipit

MEADOW PIPIT
Anthus pratensis L14cm

Characteristics: A slim and rather long-tailed insectivorous bird with mostly brown plumage. The upperparts are mostly plain brown with an olive tinge and the paler underside is streaked with brown on the breast. The dark flesh-pink legs are a useful field characteristic for separating this species from the Tree Pipit and the calls are also distinctive. The Meadow Pipit makes a 'tseep' call, often repeated three or four times, and its song is usually delivered from a short song flight starting from the ground and not from a tree. The song starts with a few short fast notes and then increases in tempo ending as a trill.

140

Distribution and habitat: A very widespread and sometimes common resident. Nests on rough meadows, open country, moorland, dunes and coastal meadows. In winter may be much commoner on coastal marshes. A summer visitor only to northern Europe.

Habits and similar species: Feeds mainly on small insects caught on the ground or in low vegetation, and in winter takes small seeds, often feeding in mixed flocks with larks and finches. Nests on the ground making small cup of woven grasses and leaves. Tree Pipit is very similar but can be separated by song and leg colour. Rock Pipit has dark brown legs and darker greyish-olive upperparts.

Stonechat

♀

♂

imm

STONECHAT
Saxicola torquata L12.5cm

Characteristics: The male is a striking bird as it sits on top of a low bush with its black head and bright chestnut breast and white on wings, neck and rump. Females and juveniles are browner and more streaked on the upperparts. In winter the male's head becomes browner. The call is a harsh 'tchack', sounding like two stones being knocked together and is the reason for its name. The song is a short squeaky warble, somewhere between the Whitethroat's and the Dunnock's and is usually delivered from a perch but may be given from a fluttering song flight.

Distribution and habitat: A common resident on moors and heaths and coastal scrub. Mainly confined to Britain and western Europe and a summer visitor to central Europe. Nest is well hidden in thick vegetation such as gorse or heather, often very low down.

Habits and similar species: Feeds mostly on insects and spiders caught in low vegetation. May take tiny fruits and berries in autumn. Whinchat lacks black head and has prominent eye-stripe. Black Redstart is mostly black without chestnut breast.

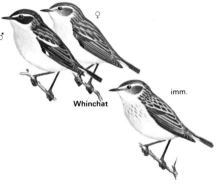

Whinchat

♀

♂

imm.

WHINCHAT
Saxicola rubetra L12.5cm
Characteristics: Distinguished from Stonechat by the white eye-stripe and white patches on the tail which show well in flight. The upperparts are streaked brown and the underside is a warm orange-buff. Females are similar to males but the colours are more subdued. The song is a series of short and quiet warbles and is rather intermittent; it may be heard at night. The alarm call is a rapid ticking 'u tic' or 'tic tic'.

Distribution and habitat: Common summer visitor to heaths, rough grassland, riverside meadows, open country with scattered bushes. Very widespread, but often absent from large tracts of countryside. A common passage migrant at many coastal sites.

Habits and similar species: Mainly an insect feeder but takes small berries in autumn just before migration. Nests on the ground near a grass tussock or low bush, making a cup of finely woven grasses lined with hair. Often seen perching on low bush or thistle, frequently flicking tail. Redstart has black face and chin with white forehead and no eye-stripe, and its tail is red with no white patches.

141

NIGHTJAR
Caprimulgus europaeus L28cm
Characteristics: An extremely difficult bird to see due to its excellent camouflage. By day it sits on the ground blending with dead leaves. Easily detected at night by its characteristic churring call which can be very prolonged, sounds at times as if changing gear; also makes a 'chuck' sound.

Distribution and habitat: A fairly local breeding bird on dry heaths, young conifer plantations and open woodlands. Occurs over most of Britain and Europe apart from far north. Nests on the ground in a shallow scrape, using no nesting material.

Habits and similar species: Catches night-flying moths and other insects at dusk and through the night. May rest on the ground or on a dead branch. A late-arriving migrant and one of the earliest to leave. Red-necked Nightjar is confined to extreme south-west Europe and has sandier colours and more white on throat. The song is a prolonged di-syllabic 'kerchuck kerchuck kerchuck'.

TOWNS AND GARDENS

Some birds have long been familiar to man, living at such close proximity to human habitations that this is reflected in the names; the House Sparrow and House Martin have become fully adapted to living near humans, usually nesting on houses and not often found living far away from them. House Sparrows may have followed early farmers, living on spilt grain and taking animal food, but now they take a variety of foods, many of them provided for them in garden feeders. Swifts are invariably found nesting on buildings as natural nesting sites such as cliffs are extremely rare.

Some species of woodland birds have adapted well to life in gardens and have learnt to feed and nest in man-made habitats. Garden bird feeders are now an important factor influencing the survival of several species in harsh winters.

Town dwelling birds are not safe from predators, as Kestrels, Sparrowhawks, Tawny Owls and Foxes all occur in towns and gardens. In addition, town birds have to contend with domestic cats and dogs. Cats account for millions of birds each year, many of them fledglings unable to fly properly. Dogs do not often catch birds, but have a significant effect on the breeding success of ground-nesting birds, as they run the risk of frequent disturbance.

In winter towns may be appreciably warmer than the surrounding countryside, especially at night and large numbers of birds fly in from their feeding grounds to roost communally in warmer conditions. Starlings sometimes form flocks numbering millions and darken the sky as they fly in to roost. Tall buildings are good substitutes for steep cliffs and Feral Pigeons, descendants of the wild Rock Dove of the coast, nest happily on high rise buildings. Kestrels may nest on window ledges, oblivious to the traffic below or the office workers behind the glass; roadside verges and railway embankments will provide them with plenty of food in the form of voles, mice and small birds.

Collared Doves on a roof; these birds are now common in towns and villages.

Kestrel

hovering

♂

♀

KESTREL
Falco tinnunculus L32-35cm

Characteristics: The only small bird of prey likely to be seen hovering for long periods. The male is reddish-brown with a grey tail and paler underparts. The larger female is a more streaked brown all over and has a reddish barred tail. When hovering the tail is fanned out and depressed slightly, but in direct flight it looks quite long. Kestrels are not normally fast fliers and do not often attempt to catch flying birds.

Distribution and habitat: Common and widespread bird in a great range of habitats; very familiar along roadsides and in towns. A summer visitor to far northern Europe and Scandinavia. Nests in abandoned bird's nests, holes in trees, rock ledges, on buildings or nest boxes.

Habits and similar species: Hunts for small mammals, especially voles, by hovering over rough grassland. Also takes small birds, beetles and reptiles. Lesser Kestrel is restricted to southern Europe and is slightly smaller. Male has unspotted upperparts and does not have a dark moustachial stripe. Both sexes have flesh-coloured, not black, claws. Nests colonially and catches flying insects on the wing.

House martin

HOUSE MARTIN
Delichon urbica L12.5cm

Characteristics: The prominent white rump is the best distinction, coupled with the brilliant white underparts and short slightly-forked tail. The upperparts are a glossy blue-black and the legs have a trousered appearance due to fluffy white feathers. The usual call is a quiet 'chirrip' and the song is a squeaky twittering medley sometimes delivered from a perch and sometimes in flight. The flight is more fluttery than the swallow's and is interspersed with elegant glides.

Distribution and habitat: A common summer visitor to all of Britain and Europe except for the extreme north. Common in towns, and in open country where there are buildings to nest on. Hunts over open country and water, catching flying insects on the wing.

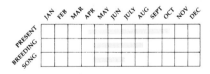

Habits and similar species: Nests under eaves and sometimes on natural cliffs, often in small colonies in sites used year after year. Builds a cup out of mud pellets and leaves only a small entrance. Swallow lacks white rump and has long deeply-forked tail. Crag Martin and Sand Martin both hunt over water, but have sandy upperparts and no white rump.

Hoopoe

imm.

HOOPOE
Upupa epops L28cm
Characteristics: Despite its striking appearance this can be a difficult bird to see as its black and white wings and salmon-pink body blend well with the rough ground it prefers to feed on. When hopping around on grass it is much more obvious, although the large crest is not always held erect. In flight it gives the appearance of an enormous black and white moth. The call sounds rather like a cross between a Tawny Owl and a Cuckoo, being a monotone 'poop poop poop'.

Distribution and habitat: A vagrant to Britain, although it has bred in the south. Often seen on lawns in large gardens and parks in the spring. Breeds in southern and central Europe in open country, gardens, orchards, olive groves and open woodland.

Habits and similar species: Feeds on insects and lizards, mostly collected from the ground. Frequently hops along furrows in recently cultivated areas. Nests in tree holes or rock crevices, using little or no nest material. Fairly shy, not often allowing a close approach, and flies off if disturbed; flight is swooping and often low over ground, giving impression of much larger bird due to broad wings.

Black redstart

♂

♀

BLACK REDSTART
Phoenicurus ochruros L14cm
Characteristics: The male is nearly all black except for his rust-red tail and white wing panel. Females more like female Redstart but darker, especially below. Alarm call a short 'tsip'. The song is a short melodious warble followed by a short pause and then a strange crackling sound followed by more of the musical notes. It is usually delivered from a perch high on a building at night or at dawn.

Distribution and habitat: A scarce summer visitor to Britain with a few overwintering. Resident in south west Europe and a summer visitor to central Europe. Common in towns and gardens in Europe, and also on rock faces, usually in very large buildings in Britain.

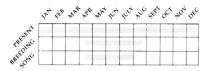

Habits and similar species: Feeds on insects and spiders, but takes small berries in autumn. Nests on ledges or in cavities, sometimes in large buildings like power stations. Redstart has grey back, white forehead and red breast. Females are very similar, but female Redstart is paler, especially below.

Robin

imm.

ROBIN
Erithacus rubecula L14cm
Characteristics: Adults of both sexes have rusty red breast, face and forehead. Juveniles are brown with dense yellow-brown spotting; they moult into adult plumage by the end of their first summer. The song, sometimes delivered from a low perch or from a more prominent position, is a pleasant musical warble, but the autumn and winter variant is more melancholy. A rapid 'tic tic tic' call is given from dense cover; also a thin, high 'tsee'.

Distribution and habitat: A very common and widespread resident of woodlands, parks, gardens and scrub. Migratory in northern and eastern parts of its range. Many are trapped and killed as they pass through Mediterranean countries in winter.

Habits and similar species: A retiring bird in its habits, but not shy of humans. Feeds on insects and small seeds and berries, often hopping along the ground. Nests in holes, ivy-covered trees and open nesting boxes, making a domed construction of leaves lined with finer material. Male Red-breasted Flycatcher also has red breast, but is smaller, has black and white tail and grey head and is scarce visitor.

146

Collared dove

COLLARED DOVE
Streptopelia decaocto L32cm
Characteristics: A small dove with mainly light colourings. In flight the tail shows a large area of white underneath and looks long and the wings show dark tips. The collar is only a partial black band around the back of the neck and is absent in juveniles. The flight is fast and direct. The call is a loud tri-syllabic 'doo-dooh-do' with the accent on the second syllable and it is often given from high prominent perches. A squealing 'kreee' call is often given by birds flying in to settle.

Distribution and habitat: A coloniser from the Balkans, rapidly spreading across Europe and reaching Britain in 1955. Now very widespread and common almost everywhere. Live mainly in towns, villages and near farms with grain stores.

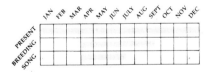

Habits and similar species: Feeds on seeds, especially spilled grain, and leaves. Nests in buildings or trees, making a flimsy platform of twigs. May start breeding as early as March and still be rearing young in November having raised two or three broods in the year. Turtle Dove is smaller and has darker markings, no neck ring and black tail with white border.

Song thrush

SONG THRUSH
Turdus philomelos L23cm
Characteristics: A uniformly brown thrush above and heavily spotted below. In flight the light orange underwing can be seen. The song is loud and musical and consists of several distinct phrases repeated two or three times; there may also be some mimicry. A sharp 'tsit' call is given from cover and there is a more frantic alarm call given if a predator such as a Sparrowhawk is seen. Hops or runs on the ground sometimes pausing with head on one side when searching for worms.

Distribution and habitat: A common and widespread resident throughout much of Europe in gardens, parks, open woodlands and hedgerows. Migratory in the northern and eastern parts of its range; many are killed by hunters in the Mediterranean.

	JAN	FEB	MAR	APR	MAY	JUN	JULY	AUG	SEPT	OCT	NOV	DEC
PRESENT												
BREEDING												
SONG												

Habits and similar species: Feeds on seeds and berries, catches earthworms and soil invertebrates and feeds on snails by cracking open the shells on an anvil. Nests in a bush or tree making a deep cup of woven grasses and moss lined with mud. Mistle Thrush is larger and has white underwing. Redwing is slightly smaller and has rusty-red underwing and white supercilium and cheek stripe.

Blackbird

♂

♀

BLACKBIRD
Turdus merula L24cm
Characteristics: The male is easily recognised by its all-black plumage and yellow bill and eye ring. Females are almost uniformly brown with dark mottlings. The song is rich and fluty, but not repetitive like the Song Thrush and not as clear as the Mistle Thrush. Each phrase ends more quietly than it started. The alarm call is an indignant sounding 'chook' or sometimes 'pink' and the calls often run together into a more frantic shriek when mobbing a predator.

Distribution and habitat: A very common and widespread resident over most of Europe except for the far north where it is migratory. Found in a great range of habitats from moorlands down to sea-level, where there is some degree of tree cover. Especially fond of gardens.

	JAN	FEB	MAR	APR	MAY	JUN	JULY	AUG	SEPT	OCT	NOV	DEC
PRESENT												
BREEDING												
SONG												

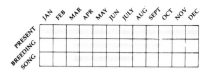

Habits and similar species: Takes a wide range of foods, but mainly earthworms and soil invertebrates, and also feeds on seeds and berries. Nests in thick bushes, trees, and open nest boxes. Builds an untidy cup of grasses, mosses and mud, with an inner grass lining. May nest very early in the year. Ring Ousel is also black but has white crescent on neck; beware partial albino blackbirds.

Mistle thrush

MISTLE THRUSH
Turdus viscivorous L28cm

Characteristics: A large thrush, heavily spotted below and with grey-brown upperparts. Outer tail feathers have white tips and underwing is white, although these features are only seen in flight. The song is similar to the Blackbird's but has a wilder air to it. The individual phrases are shorter and sung at a faster speed and the pauses between them are shorter. Does not join in the dawn chorus with other thrushes, preferring to sing during the day, and even in the rain, and then may be the dominant bird singing. A harsh rattle is the usual call.

Distribution and habitat: A common resident of open woodland, parks, gardens and cultivated areas. In winter may gather with other thrushes in open fields. Resident over a very wide area, but only a summer visitor to northern and eastern Europe.

Habits and similar species: Takes a great variety of foods, especially earthworms, insects and berries. Builds its cup-shaped nest in the fork of a tree, often quite high up. Defends the nest vigorously against intruders, including cats and humans, otherwise a fairly shy and wary bird. Song Thrush is smaller and slimmer with warmer colourings. Fieldfare is slightly smaller with grey head and rump.

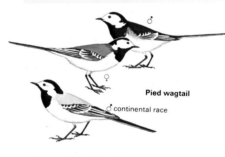

Pied wagtail
♂ continental race

PIED WAGTAIL
Motacilla alba yarellii L18.5cm

Characteristics: Much of the body length is made up of the constantly wagging tail which is black with a white border. Males have a black back and females can sometimes be picked out as they have a greyer back. Juveniles have a grey face and a grey patch on the breast. The flight note is a clear high-pitched 'chizz-ik' and there is also a one-note 'chik'. The song is a twittering version of the calls and may be delivered from the ground, a perch or the air and is sometimes given when other birds are being chased away. The flight is deeply undulating.

Distribution and habitat: A common and widespread bird breeding near water, in towns, large gardens, farms and open country. May gather in large roosts outside breeding season. Nests in crevices or ivy, making an untidy cup of grasses lined with hair and feathers.

Habits and similar species: An active lively bird, constantly running around, flicking its tail and bobbing its head. Catches insects by chasing after them and sometimes making short fly-catching flights, and also takes very small seeds in winter. White Wagtail, *Motacilla alba alba*, is European race of Pied Wagtail and has a grey, not black rump and back, contrasting with black nape.

Chaffinch

CHAFFINCH
Fringilla coelebs L15cm
Characteristics: The male is easily recognised by the combination of blue-grey head and pinkish-brown underparts. The female lacks these brighter colours being mostly a more subdued brown, but still has the double white wing bar and the white-edged tail like the male. In winter the male's colours are slightly less bright. The call is a loud almost metallic 'pink' and the flight call is a quieter 'cheup'. The song heard in spring is a descending scale of about 12 notes speeding up and ending with a flourish.

Distribution and habitat: A very common resident occurring in a wide range of habitats and over a great area, the only requirement being some trees or bushes. Upland forests, woodlands, farms, parks and gardens of all sizes are suitable habitat.

	JAN	FEB	MAR	APR	MAY	JUN	JULY	AUG	SEPT	OCT	NOV	DEC
PRESENT												
BREEDING												
SONG												

Habits and similar species: Feeds on seeds and in summer takes insects. Has learnt to visit bird tables and in parks becomes quite confiding. May gather in mixed flocks with other finches in winter. Nests in bushes or in small tree branches, making a neat cup of grasses and leaves, with lichens on the outside and a hair lining inside. Brambling has grey head in winter but has white rump and orange buff underparts.

Goldfinch
imm

GOLDFINCH
Carduelis carduelis L12cm
Characteristics: Red face and black and white head make for easy recognition. Most of the body is buff coloured, but wings are black with a bright yellow wing bar, very clearly seen in flight. Sexes almost identical, very difficult to distinguish in the field. Juveniles lack head colours of adults and are more streaked, but have yellow wing bars. The song is a pleasant-sounding series of notes similar to the 'tswitt-witt-witt' flight calls; the call is a harsher-sounding 'geez'.

Distribution and habitat: A common and widespread resident over most of Britain and Europe except the far north. A summer visitor to the eastern parts of its range. Common in open country with trees and bushes, gardens and waste ground.

	JAN	FEB	MAR	APR	MAY	JUN	JULY	AUG	SEPT	OCT	NOV	DEC
PRESENT												
BREEDING												
SONG												

Habits and similar species: Very fond of the seeds of thistles and teasels, but takes many other types of seeds in season. Nests in a thick bush or the outermost twigs of a tree making a neat cup of grasses lined with hair. May be very secretive in breeding season, but in winter gathers in small flocks and is much more obvious. Many migrate south in winter and large numbers are trapped in the Mediterranean.

Greenfinch

GREENFINCH
Carduelis chloris L14.5cm
Characteristics: Adult male is bright yellow-green below and olive-green above; the colours are brightest in summer. Females are duller with more grey and brown colouring; juveniles are greyish-green and brown and streaked. In all plumages there are bright yellow areas on the tail and wings. The song is a mixture of twittering notes interspersed with a nasal 'dzeeee'. This may be given from a tree-top or during a short fluttering flight out from a high perch. Normal flight calls are a few soft quiet notes.

Distribution and habitat: A very common and widespread resident over most of Britain and Europe, and a summer visitor to northern Europe and Scandinavia. Found in most open areas with trees, hedgerows, parks as well as gardens.

Habits and similar species: Feeds mainly on seeds and is a regular visitor to bird tables. Nests in shrubs or low trees, sometimes in loose colonies, building a lined cup of mosses and twigs. May raise 2 broods in a good seed year. Siskin is smaller and male has black crown and black and yellow wing bars. Serin is even smaller, has yellower breast and more streaked upperparts with yellow rump.

Bullfinch

BULLFINCH
Pyrrhula pyrrhula L16cm
Characteristics: Both sexes have black crown, wings and tail, grey upperparts, white rump and white wing bar. The male has red underparts, but female is dull grey brown. Bill is short and heavy. Juveniles resemble females but without black head. A very quiet bird, but a soft insipid 'pew' or 'pee-u' call is made by birds usually hidden from view. The song is very weak and tuneless and consists of a few calls and nasal notes.

Distribution and habitat: A common and widespread resident absent only from the far north and very high altitudes. Occurs wherever there are seed-bearing trees; farmland, orchards, mixed woodland and gardens. Nests in a dense bush, making a shallow cup.

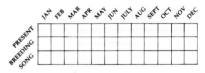

Habits and similar species: Feeds mainly on seeds, but will eat buds of fruit trees in spring. Usually only seen in pairs, but may gather in small loose flocks in winter; very shy and retiring. Hawfinch also has large bill, but it is much larger and male plumage lacks red colours. Pine Grosbeak is rare vagrant to Britain and has large bill, red colours in male but no black head, white rump or white wing bars.

Linnet

LINNET
Carduelis cannabina L13.5cm
Characteristics: The male is easily recognised by its grey head, red breast and crown and rich brown back. Females and juveniles are dull brown with darker streaks. Both sexes have prominent silvery-white panels in the wing and a pale streaked throat. The male's colours are less vivid in winter. The song is a pleasant twittering collection of short phrases, often given in chorus from the top of a bush or other prominent song-post. There are many calls and flocks of birds are usually very vocal making a variety of 'tsweet' sounds.

Distribution and habitat: A common and widespread resident on open country with scattered bushes, especially gorse, and in

winter common on agricultural land, large gardens, wasteland with thick vegetation. Nests semi-colonially in dense bushes such as gorse.

Habits and similar species: Feeds mainly on small seeds, some collected from the plants themselves and some from the ground. Usually in small flocks, joining with other finches and buntings in autumn to feed on stubble fields when flocks may reach enormous size. Twite is same size and build but lacks the bright colourings and wing bars and is more northerly in its range.

Serin

SERIN
Serinus serinus L11.5cm
Characteristics: A very small finch with a short stout bill and a yellow rump. Males have the brightest colours with a yellow head and breast and females and juveniles have more drab colours with more streaking below. In summer when the feathers become worn and lose the greyish-green edges, the head can appear almost completely yellow. The flight call is a fast trilling 'zrr-litt'. The song is delivered from a high song-post or from a fluttering song flight. It is a musical jingling medley with some nasal sounds slightly reminiscent of Corn Bunting.

Distribution and habitat: A very scarce summer visitor and breeding bird in Britain, but more widespread in southern

and central Europe, inhabiting open woodland, parks and gardens. Nests in a dense tree, sometimes conifers, building a well-concealed cup of grass.

Habits and similar species: Feeds on seeds and some insects in summer. Siskin is slightly larger and has black head and longer bill with more prominent yellow wing bars. Citril Finch is confined to high mountain conifer forests and has plain, unstreaked, yellowish-green underparts and rump.

Waxwing

Distribution and habitat:

A winter visitor to Britain and central Europe from its breeding grounds in Scandinavia and northern Europe. Numbers depend on winter weather and food supplies; mass irruptions occur in some years. Breeds in far northern forests nesting in small trees.

WAXWING
Bombycilla garrulus L18cm
Characteristics: A plump light brown bird with a prominent crest. The wings have red tips on the inner feathers, looking like tiny drops of sealing wax. The plumage is mostly plain, but the under-tail coverts are red and the tip of the tail is yellow. The rump is grey. Juveniles lack the crest and black chin and are slightly streaked below. Waxwings are normally silent but they can produce a high trilling 'sirrr'.

Habits and similar species: Feeds on berries and fruits, often attracted to shrubs and trees with clusters of bright red berries. Feeds voraciously for a short time then retires to a perch to digest its meal. Often very confiding and very likely to be encountered in the middle of a town if berry-bearing bushes are present. May roost on television aerials or bare branches when not feeding.

152

House sparrow

♂ summer

Distribution and habitat:

Strongly associated with human habitation and spread over a very wide area, but only where there are villages, farms or towns. Absent only from Iceland and the extreme north. Nests colonially, usually in buildings, but will use bushes or trees.

HOUSE SPARROW
Passer domesticus L14.5cm
Characteristics: A familiar species of towns and gardens, the male very easily recognised by his black bib, grey crown and rump, chestnut mantle and white wing bar. Females and juveniles are much plainer with an unstreaked breast and a pale supercilium. The call and the song are a monotonous series of chirps and cheeps, and sometimes a di-syllabic 'chizzick'. These calls may sometimes be joined into a sort of song and may be given in chorus by a group of birds hopping around on a building.

Habits and similar species: Feeds mostly on plant material, seeds, spilt grain and is a regular and noisy visitor to bird tables. Takes some insect food in summer. May raise up to 3 broods in a year. Spanish Sparrow is restricted to south-west Europe and Balkans and has far greater extent of black on breast and chestnut head.

Starling

♂ summer

winter

STARLING
Sturnus vulgaris L21.5cm
Characteristics: A noisy and gregarious bird with glossy, speckled, mostly black plumage. The bill is long and pointed and noticeably pale. The tail is short and this with the pointed wings gives a triangular outline in flight. The flight call is a short 'cherrr', and the song is a chattering medley containing much convincing mimicry. It may include elements of many other birds' songs plus unnatural sounds like doorbells. Runs on the ground in search of food but does not make long pauses like thrushes.

Distribution and habitat: A very common and widespread bird found over most of Britain and Europe. In the north of its range it is only a summer visitor and in the winter there is a definite migration south and west. Nests in tree holes, crevices, buildings.

Habits and similar species: Feeds on insects and other invertebrates often taken from the ground. May gather in huge flocks numbering many thousands of birds and roost in city centres, reed beds or forests. Spotless Starling is confined to south-west Europe; has plain black plumage in summer but is spotted in winter. Rose-coloured Starling has pink body and shaggy black head; a visitor from the Middle East.

153

Jackdaw

juv.

JACKDAW
Corvus monedula L33cm
Characteristics: The smallest of the black crows and the only black landbird with a grey nape and a grey eye. The 'chack' call is repeated many times by roosting birds and a harsher 'kow' call is also given as birds take to the air. In flight the wingbeats are powerful and fast with the wings looking more rounded than in other crows. Very sociable and always seen in flocks. May circle high up, performing elaborate aerobatics. In autumn may gather in very large flocks to roost in towns and engages in mass noisy flight displays before dark.

Distribution and habitat: A common and widespread resident over most of Europe except for the far north and only a summer visitor to the extreme northern and eastern parts of its range. Occurs in many habitats, including farmland, parks, towns and sea-cliffs.

Habits and similar species: A gregarious bird feeding in large noisy flocks on invertebrates, seeds and sometimes refuse. Nests in colonies on buildings, tree holes, crevices or burrows on cliffs. Chough also occurs on sea cliffs but has all black plumage and bill is long, downcurved and red. Hooded Crow is much larger and has greater extent of pale grey on back and underside.

Swift

SWIFT
Apus apus L17cm

Characteristics: The most aerial of all birds, spending almost its entire life in the air apart from its time in the nest as a nestling or brooding adult. The long, narrow scythe-like wings, streamlined body and short tail give the Swift its dashing outline in flight and separate it easily from the swallows and martins. Makes screaming calls as it flies in groups very high or with great accuracy over rooftops.

Distribution and habitat: Occurs over a very wide range, often leaving one area in bad weather and travelling a great distance to find food. Most often found near towns and villages. Nests under eaves, in church towers, houses and very rarely in trees.

Habits and similar species: Catches insects on the wing by flying at great speed with gaping mouth. Nests often contain many fleas and feather lice. Young may be left for long periods as adults go on long feeding forays; they may enter a state of torpor until the parents return. Alpine Swift is larger (L23cm) with white underside and brown breast-band, and is confined to southern Europe.

GLOSSARY

bird of prey bird with talons and hooked bill. Members of the orders Falconi-
formes and Strigiformes
breeding plumage distinctive plumage of a bird in the breeding season. Also
called 'nuptial plumage'
carrion carcases of animals, eaten by some species but not killed by them
clutch set of eggs laid by one female and brooded together
cup-nest hemispherical nest open at the top
diurnal active during daylight
down very fine feathers which help to trap air and keep the bird warm
eclipse moult which ducks undergo during the latter part of the summer
first winter plumage feathers a young bird grows in its first autumn moult,
replacing the juvenile plumage
fledged young birds are said to have 'fledged' when they can fly and have
left the nest
immature young bird which has passed the 'nestling' stage but has not yet
reached full adulthood
jizz birdwatcher's term for the combination of shape and movement by
which a bird may be identified
juvenile young bird which has its first real feathers after it has passed the
'nestling' stage and before it is described as an 'immature'
juvenile plumage young bird's first feathers which push out the natal down.
They are replaced in the autumn of the first year by the bird's first winter
plumage
lek display gatherings of some species during breeding time, at which the
males display to one another and drive off other males
migrant species that moves from one area to another at different times of the
year
nestling one of the words used to describe a bird until it is full-grown and
able to fly
nidicolous describes young birds which remain in the nest after hatching
nidifugous describes young birds which leave the nest soon after hatching
passage migrants birds which stop temporarily on their migration journey
passerines birds of the order Passeriformes (perching birds); the largest of all
orders of birds
pellet the hard lump of indigestible pieces of food, which a bird regurgitates
preening method of feather care in which the bird draws the feathers, base
first, through its bill. This has the effect of cleaning off dirt and lice and also
fits the barbs and barbules into place
prey animals which are taken for food by other animals
ringing method of marking a bird by fixing a light metal or plastic ring to
its leg in order to compile records of migration, mortality rate, and so on
sedentary describes a bird which does not move very far over the course of
a year
songpost prominent perches round the perimeter of a bird's terrritory, from
which it will sing to announce its ownership to possible intruders
sub-species population of species that is different from other populations of
the same species but which will interbreed. (Carrion Crows and Hooded
Crows look different but they interbreed where populations overlap. There-
fore they are the same speces.)
territory area which a particular bird occupies and defends against other
birds of the same species
vagrant bird which occurs in a particular place accidentally, due to storms,
cloud and other adverse weather conditions. Also called accidental

INDEX

156

159

PHOTOGRAPHIC ACKNOWLEDGEMENTS

Nature Photographers = NP

Frank Blackburn/NP 73 top, 141 bottom; Ola Bondesson 49 bottom, 130 bottom, 136 top; N A Calow/NP 81 top; Kevin Carlson/NP 13, 71 top, 77 top, 98 bottom; Colin Carver/NP 28 bottom, 154 bottom; Hugh Clark/NP 10, 54-55; Andrew Cleave/NP 15; Dave Cottridge 20 bottom; Thomas Ennis/NP 52 bottom; Pekko Helo 58 top; Eric & David Hosking 45 top; Chris & Jo Knights/NP 59 bottom, 107 top, 120 bottom; Urban Olsson 30 top; W S Paton/NP 84-85; Paul Sterry/NP 16-17, 26 top, 50 bottom, 83 top, 114 top; Roger Tidman/NP 9, 33 bottom, 70 bottom, 128-129, 144-145; Maurice Walker/NP 93 bottom, 112-113.